金原瑞人
MY FAVORITES

ALBERT CAMUS

THE STRANGER

異邦人

アルベール・カミュ

青灯社

まえがき

1．フランス語の作品を英訳で読む？

翻訳を始めてもう25年くらいになるが、英語から日本語への翻訳はじつに難しい。それにくらべれば、英語からフランス語、ドイツ語からスペイン語、スペイン語から英語などの翻訳はじつに楽だ……というのは言い過ぎかもしれないが、それでも英語↔日本語の翻訳と比べるとはるかに楽なのはまちがいない。なにしろ、ヨーロッパの言語はラテン系だゲルマン系だとかいっても、所詮はみんな親戚同士だ。

たとえば、同時通訳の方からこんなことをうかがったことがある。

「英語から日本語への同時通訳は非常に疲れる。内容にもよるが、ふたり交替で通訳をしていてもしんどいことがあるくらいだ。それにひきかえ、ヨーロッパの言葉同士の通訳なんて、びっくりするくらい楽。こないだ英語をフランス語に同時通訳していたおばさんなんか、編み物しながらやってた」

多少の誇張はあるにせよ、そのくらいの差はあると思う。

文の構造や単語がどれくらい異なっているか、どれくらい似ているか、それを考えるだけで違いはわかってもらえると思う。ということは、通訳も翻訳もずいぶん無理をしているということだ。無理をしているということは、オリジナルからどうしても、はずれてしまう、ずれてしまう、離れてしまう、ということ。通訳も訳者も、なるべくそれを少なくするよう必死の努力をする……のだが、なんのなんの、日本語とヨーロッパの言葉の壁は高くて厚い。

その点、ヨーロッパ言語同士の場合、その壁がないとはいわないが、比較的、低くて薄い。

ということは、訳者の力量などにもよるだろうが一般的にいって、ヨーロッパ言語の作品は日本語訳より英訳のほうがオリジナルに近い。

論より証拠で、『異邦人』の最初のページから一部分、フランス語の原文と、その英語訳を抜き出してみよう。

L'asile de vieillards est à Marengo, à quatre-vingts kilomètres d'Alger. Je prendrai l'autobus à 2 heures et j'arriverai dans l'après-midi. Ainsi, je pourrai veiller et je rentrerai demain soir. J'ai demandé deux jours de congé à mon patron et il ne pouvait pas me les refuser avec une excuse pareille. Mais il n'avait pas l'air content. Je lui ai même dit : « Ce n'est pas de ma faute. » Il n'a pas répondu.

The old people's home is at Marengo, about eighty kilometers from Algiers, I'll take the two o'clock bus and get there in the afternoon. That way I can be there for the vigil and come back tomorrow night. I asked my boss for two days off and there was no way he was going to refuse me with an excuse like that. But he wasn't too happy about it. I even said, "It's not my fault." He didn't say anything.

ほぼ１：１の対応ではないか。

なら、英語の好きな人や英語のできる人は、ヨーロッパ言語の作品を読みたければ日本語訳ではなく英訳で読めばいい。英語の勉強をしたい人にも勧めたい。これには次のようなメリットがある。

①日本語訳よりは原作に近いものを読める。

②日本語訳で読むより時間がかかるぶん、細かくじっくり読むことになり、理解が広がる。

③英語力がつく。

そんなわけで、アルベール・カミュの『異邦人』の英訳本（Matthew Ward 訳・VINTAGE INTERNATIONAL）に語注をつけてみた。ただし、高校や大学のリーダーのテキストとちがって、文法的な説明は最小限にとどめた。それは英文を読むのに文法は必要ないからではない。文法は言語の約束事をコンパクトにまとめた道具で、旅行をするときの地図のようなものだ。しっかりした地図を持っているかどうかは旅に大きく影響する。しかし、この本の目的は、英文と注をうまく使いながら、作品を読み、味わうことなので、文法的な説明は少なくしてある。

２．文法について

語注では文法にはほとんど触れていないが、いくつか注意してほしいことがあるので、少しだけ書いておきたい。

「使える英語」とかいう意味不明の言葉が流行し始めて以来、英語の授業は文法や読解の時間が減って、いまや会話中心になってしまった。しかし、小説やエッセイでは口語であまり使われない表現がよく出てくる。

たとえば分詞構文。これは用法が多岐にわたっているので、ここでは説明しないが、不安な方はぜひこれを機会に、文法や読解の参考書を読んで勉強してほしい。

それからもうひとつ、It is (was)...that の強調構文も会話ではあまり使われないので、苦手な人が多い。この『異邦人』の英訳にはよく出てくるので、簡単に説明しておこう。

たとえば "He met Marie yesterday."「彼は昨日、マリーに会った」という文のうち、'he' 'Marie' 'yesterday' の3つをそれぞれ強調したい場合、次のように表現する。

・It was he that met Marie yesterday.（昨日マリーに会ったのは彼だ）

・It was Marie that he met yesterday.（彼が昨日会ったのはマリーだ）

・It was yesterday that he met Marie.（彼がマリーに会ったのは昨日だ）

It is (was)...that の強調構文を、It が that 以下を受けていると勘違いすると意味がわからなくなるので注意してほしい。この強調構文、上の例のように単純な場合は気がつきやすいが、文が長くなったり複雑になったりすると、案外と難しい。この註釈本では何カ所か、指摘しておいた。

それから会話でほとんど使われないが、小説などでは描出話法もよく使われる。たとえば、この本でいえば、242ページの8行目にこんな文がある。

I was pouring out on him everything that was in my heart, cries of anger and cries of joy.
（私は彼に、心のなかにあるものすべてをぶちまけた。それは怒りの叫びであり、喜びの叫びだった）

そしてそのあと、こう続く。

He seemed so certain about everything, didn't he? And yet none of his certainties was worth one hair of a woman's head...

これをそのまま訳すとこんな感じになる。「彼はすべてのことについて自信があるようにみえた、そうではないか？　しかし彼の自信は女の頭の髪の毛一本ほどにもあたいしない」
しかし、これは描出話法であって、私（主人公）が、彼にぶちまけた言葉なのだ。だから次のようになる。「あんたは、なんでも自信があるらしいな？　だが、あんたの自信なんて、女の頭の髪の毛一本ほどにもあたいしないんだ」
これがわかっていないと、とんでもない間違いを犯してしまうので要注意。
It is (was)...that の強調構文も、描出話法も、会話ではあまり使われることはないが、小説だけでなく、いろんな文章でよく使われる。

インターネットがこれほどまでに普及してきた現代、「使える英語」は会話よりも、読み書きのほうにシフトしてきている。しっかり、いろんな文章を読んで、英語を読むというのがどういうことなのか、実感してほしいと思う。

文法的なことで、もうひとつ。これは会話でも書き言葉でもよく使われるので覚えておいてほしい。それは一般人称の 'you' だ。この 'you' は「きみ、あなた」という意味はまったくなく、'one' とか 'they' とか 'we' にあたる。

たとえば、こんなふうに使われる。

・You should be careful when you say 'I love you.'

（「愛している」っていうときには、気をつけなくちゃ）

・The older you get, the more you learn about life. (人は年をとればとるほど、人生について多くを学ぶようになる。年を取れば、人生がわかってくるよ)

一般人称の 'you' については、いくつか注で指摘しておいたが、その他にもあるので、みつけてみてほしい。

3．『異邦人』の舞台、その他について

舞台は、冒頭にも書かれているように、アルジェリア。

アルジェリアは現在のアルジェリア民主人民共和国で、首都はアルジェ。アフリカ大陸の北西部にあり、地中海に面している。日本人にとってなじみのあるのは、サハラ砂漠くらいかもしれない。

この国は1830年から1962年までフランスの植民地だった。『異邦人』は1939年頃から執筆され、42年にフランスの老舗、ガリマール書店から出版された。いうまでもなく、フランスの植民地時代のアルジェリアが舞台だ。

そんなところで生まれ育ったムルソーが、「陽射しが強かったから」という理由で、現地のアラブ人を殺し、その罪で裁かれることになる小説、まずは最後までゆっくり味わいながら読んでみてほしい。

金原瑞人

contents

装幀　眞島和馬

The Stranger

PART ONE

1

Maman died today. Or yesterday maybe, I don't know. I got a telegram from the home: "Mother deceased. Funeral tomorrow. Faithfully yours." That doesn't mean anything. Maybe it was yesterday.

The old people's home is at Marengo, about eighty kilometers from Algiers, I'll take the two o'clock bus and get there in the afternoon. That way I can be there for the vigil and come back tomorrow night. I asked my boss for two days off and there was no way he was going to refuse me with an excuse like that. But he wasn't too happy about it. I even said, "It's not my fault." He didn't say anything. Then I thought I shouldn't have said that. After all, I didn't have anything to apologize for. He's the one who should have offered his condolences. But he probably will day after tomorrow, when he sees I'm in mourning. For now, it's almost as if Maman weren't dead. After the funeral, though, the case will be closed, and everything will have a more official feel to it.

I caught the two o'clock bus. It was very hot. I ate at the restaurant, at Céleste's, as usual. Everybody felt very sorry for me, and Céleste said, "You only have one mother." When I left, they walked me to the door. I was a little distracted because I still had to go up to Emmanuel's place to borrow a black tie and an arm band. He lost his uncle a few months back.

I ran so as not to miss the bus. It was probably

4 **deceased** 死んだ **Funeral** 葬儀 5 **Faithfully yours** 手紙の末尾につける慣用句

7 **The old people's home** 老人ホーム **Marengo** マランゴ。現在の Hadjout（アジュー）。フランス植民地時代の旧名 8 **Algiers** アルジェ。アルジェリアの首都 9 **That way** そうすれば、それなら 10 **vigil** 通夜 11 **for two days off** 二日の休み **there was no way** このあとの he was going to 以下のようなことはありえない 12 **with an excuse like that** こんな理由があれば **wasn't too happy** いい顔をしなかった 13 **It's not my fault** 私のせいじゃありません 16 **condolences** 悔やみ 17 **he probably will** このあとに、offer his condolences と続く 18 **in mourning** 喪服を着ている **For now** 今のところは 19 **the case will be closed** この件はけりがつく 20 **official feel to it** それへの公の感情（母親が死んだということをみんながちゃんと認めること）

23 **Céleste's** セレストの店 24 **You only have one mother**（You は一般人称）。母親ってのはひとりしかいない 25 **walked me to the door** 入口まで私についてきてくれた 26 **distracted** 落ち着かなかった **Emmanuel's place** エマニュエルの部屋（主人公と同じアパートに住んでいる） 27 **an arm band** 腕に付ける喪章

29 **so as not to miss the bus** バスに乗り遅れないように **It was...that I dozed off**（強調構文）

because of all the rushing around, and on top of that the bumpy ride, the smell of gasoline, and the glare of the sky and the road, that I dozed off. I slept almost the whole way. And when I woke up, I was slumped against a soldier who smiled at me and asked if I'd been traveling long. I said, "Yes," just so I wouldn't have to say anything else.

The home is two kilometers from the village. I walked them. I wanted to see Maman right away. But the caretaker told me I had to see the director first. He was busy, so I waited awhile. The caretaker talked the whole time and then I saw the director. I was shown into his office. He was a little old man with the ribbon of the Legion of Honor in his lapel. He looked at me with his clear eyes. Then he shook my hand and held it so long I didn't know how to get it loose. He thumbed through a file and said, "Madame Meursault came to us three years ago. You were her sole support." I thought he was criticizing me for something and I started to explain. But he cut me off. "You don't have to justify yourself, my dear boy. I've read your mother's file. You weren't able to provide for her properly. She needed someone to look after her. You earn only a modest salary. And the truth of the matter is, she was happier here." I said, "Yes, sir." He added, "You see, she had friends here, people her own age. She was able to share things from the old days with them. You're young, and it must have been hard for her with you."

It was true. When she was at home with me, Maman used to spend her time following me with her eyes, not

1 **all the rushing around** 急いだこと **on top of that** そのうえに **the bumpy ride** バスが揺れること 2 **glare** まぶしさ 3 **dozed off** うとうとした 4 **slumped against** もたれていた 6 **just so I wouldn't have to say anything else** ほかになにもいわないですむように

9 **right away** すぐに **caretaker** 管理人 10 **see the director** 所長に会う 12 **was shown** 案内された 13 **the Legion of Honor** レジオンドヌール勲章（ナポレオン1世によって制定されたもので、軍事、文化、科学、商工業などに功労のあった人に与えられるフランス最高の勲章） 14 **lapel** 襟 16 **get it loose** 自分の手を放してもらう **thumbed through a file** ファイルをめくった 17 **Madame Meursault** ムルソー夫人（主人公の母親） 18 **sole support** ただひとりの身寄り 19 **cut me off** 私の言葉の途中で口をはさんだ 20 **justify yourself** 自分を正当化する（言い訳をする） 21 **provide for her properly** 母親の世話を十分にする 23 **modest salary** つつましい給料 **the truth of the matter is** 本当のところ 26 **share things from the old days with them** ここの仲間と昔のことを話し合う

saying a thing. For the first few days she was at the home she cried a lot. But that was because she wasn't used to it. A few months later and she would have cried if she'd been taken out. She was used to it. That's partly why I didn't go there much this past year. And also because it took up my Sunday—not to mention the trouble of getting to the bus, buying tickets, and spending two hours traveling.

The director spoke to me again. But I wasn't really listening anymore. Then he said, "I suppose you'd like to see your mother." I got up without saying anything and he led the way to the door. On the way downstairs, he explained, "We've moved her to our little mortuary. So as not to upset the others. Whenever one of the residents dies, the others are a bit on edge for the next two or three days. And that makes it difficult to care for them." We crossed a courtyard where there were lots of old people chatting in little groups. As we went by, the talking would stop. And then the conversation would start up again behind us. The sound was like the muffled jabber of parakeets. The director stopped at the door of a small building. "I'll leave you now, Monsieur Meursault. If you need me for anything, I'll be in my office. As is usually the case, the funeral is set for ten o'clock in the morning. This way you'll be able to keep vigil over the departed. One last thing: it seems your mother often expressed to her friends her desire for a religious burial. I've taken the liberty of making the necessary arrangements. But I wanted to let you know." I thanked

2 **cried a lot** しじゅう泣いていた　3 **used to it** それに慣れる　4 **she'd been taken out** ホームから連れもどされる　**That's partly why** その理由のひとつは why 以下だった　6 **took up my Sunday** 日曜日を取りあげることになった　**not to mention** ～はいうまでもない　7 **getting to the bus** バスに乗ること　12 **led the way to the door** ドアのところまで案内してくれた　**On the way downstairs** 階段を下りる途中で　13 **mortuary** 遺体安置所　14 **So as not to upset the others** ほかの人たちを不安にさせないように　15 **on edge** 気持ちが不安定な状態　16 **care for them** 彼らの世話をする　17 **a courtyard** 庭、中庭　18 **in little groups** 数人ずつ固まって　20 **muffled jabber of parakeets** インコのわけのわからないおしゃべり　24 **As is usually the case** しきたりとして　25 **This way** ですから　**keep vigil** お通夜をする　26 **the departed** 死者（死んだ母親）　**One last thing** 最後にひとつ　28 **burial** 埋葬　**I've taken the liberty of**（勝手に）～させてもらった　**making the necessary arrangements** 必要な処理（手続）をすること

him. While not an atheist, Maman had never in her life given a thought to religion.

I went in. It was a very bright, whitewashed room with a skylight for a roof. The furniture consisted of some chairs and some cross-shaped sawhorses. Two of them, in the middle of the room, were supporting a closed casket. All you could see were some shiny screws, not screwed down all the way, standing out against the walnut-stained planks. Near the casket was an Arab nurse in a white smock, with a brightly colored scarf on her head.

Just then the caretaker came in behind me. He must have been running. He stuttered a little. "We put the cover on, but I'm supposed to unscrew the casket so you can see her." He was moving toward the casket when I stopped him. He said, "You don't want to?" I answered, "No." He was quiet, and I was embarrassed because I felt I shouldn't have said that. He looked at me and then asked, "Why not?" but without criticizing, as if he just wanted to know. I said, "I don't know." He started twirling his moustache, and then without looking at me, again he said, "I understand." He had nice pale blue eyes and a reddish complexion. He offered me a chair and then sat down right behind me. The nurse stood up and went toward the door. At that point the caretaker said to me, "She's got an abscess." I didn't understand, so I looked over at the nurse and saw that she had a bandage wrapped around her head just below the eyes. Where her nose should have been, the bandage was flat.

1 **While not an atheist** 無神論者ではなかったものの 2 **given a thought to religion** 宗教にこだわる
3 **whitewashed** 漆喰が塗られた 4 **skylight** 天窓 **consisted of** ～などからなっていた 5 **cross-shaped sawhorses** 脚がX型の台 7 **a closed casket** ふたの閉まった棺 **shiny screws** 光っているねじ釘 8 **not screwed down all the way** ねじ込まれていない 頭のところまで（完全に） **standing out against** 突き出ている 9 **walnut-stained planks** 茶褐色の塗料を塗った板 10 **smock** 仕事着、上っ張り
13 **stuttered** 口ごもった 14 **I'm supposed to** ～することになっている **unscrew** ねじ釘を抜く 17 **I was embarrassed** 気まずい思いをした 19 **without criticizing** 非難する口調ではなく 21 **twirling his moustache** 口ひげをいじること 23 **reddish complexion** 赤味がかった顔 24 **right**（強調）ちょうど 25 **At that point** そのとき 26 **She's got an abscess** 彼女は腫れ物ができている 28 **bandage** 包帯 29 **Where her nose should have been** 鼻のあるべき場所で **flat** 平らになっている（もりあがっていない）

All you could see of her face was the whiteness of the bandage.

When she'd gone, the caretaker said, "I'll leave you alone." I don't know what kind of gesture I made, but he stayed where he was, behind me. Having this presence breathing down my neck was starting to annoy me. The room was filled with beautiful late-afternoon sunlight. Two hornets were buzzing against the glass roof. I could feel myself getting sleepy. Without turning around, I said to the caretaker, "Have you been here long?" Right away he answered, "Five years"—as if he'd been waiting all along for me to ask.

After that he did a lot of talking. He would have been very surprised if anyone had told him he would end up caretaker at the Marengo home. He was sixty-four and came from Paris. At that point I interrupted him. "Oh, you're not from around here?" Then I remembered that before taking me to the director's office, he had talked to me about Maman. He'd told me that they had to bury her quickly, because it gets hot in the plains, especially in this part of the country. That was when he told me he had lived in Paris and that he had found it hard to forget it. In Paris they keep vigil over the body for three, sometimes four days. But here you barely have time to get used to the idea before you have to start running after the hearse. Then his wife had said to him, "Hush now, that's not the sort of thing to be telling the gentleman." The old man had blushed and apologized. I'd stepped in and said, "No, not at all." I thought what he'd been

1 **All you could see of her face** 彼女の顔でみえるものといえば 5 **Having this presence breathing down my neck** この存在（管理人のこと）がすぐ後ろにいること 6 **starting** ～し始めた 8 **hornets** スズメバチ **buzzing** 羽音を立てている **against** ～にぶつかって 9 **Without turning around** ふり向かないで 10 **Right away** すぐに 12 **for me to ask** 私がたずねること 13 **He would...from Paris**（この3行ほどは、この管理人のいった言葉「昔なら、おまえはマランゴの老人ホームの管理人で終わるなんていわれたら、そりゃびっくりしただろうよ。いまは64歳だがね。パリ出身なんだ」） 14 **end up caretaker** 管理人で終わる 15 **at the Marengo home** マランゴの老人ホーム 16 **At that point** そこで、そのとき 18 **director's office** 所長のオフィス 20 **plains** 草原 23 **the body** 遺体 24 **get used to the idea** そんな考えに慣れる 25 **running after the hearse** 棺をのせた車のあとを走っていく 26 **Hush now** もう、口をつぐみなさいよ 28 **stepped in** 割って入った 29 **not at all** ちっとも

saying was interesting and made sense.

In the little mortuary he told me that he'd come to the home because he was destitute. He was in good health, so he'd offered to take on the job of caretaker. I pointed out that even so he was still a resident. He said no, he wasn't. I'd already been struck by the way he had of saying "they" or "the others" and, less often, "the old people," talking about the patients, when some of them weren't any older than he was. But of course it wasn't the same. He was the caretaker, and to a certain extent he had authority over them.

Just then the nurse came in. Night had fallen suddenly. Darkness had gathered, quickly, above the skylight. The caretaker turned the switch and I was blinded by the sudden flash of light. He suggested I go to the dining hall for dinner. But I wasn't hungry. Then he offered to bring me a cup of coffee with milk. I like milk in my coffee, so I said yes, and he came back a few minutes later with a tray. I drank the coffee. Then I felt like having a smoke. But I hesitated, because I didn't know if I could do it with Maman right there. I thought about it; it didn't matter. I offered the caretaker a cigarette and we smoked.

At one point he said, "You know, your mother's friends will be coming to keep vigil too. It's customary. I have to go get some chairs and some black coffee." I asked him if he could turn off one of the lights. The glare on the white walls was making me drowsy. He said he couldn't. That was how they'd been wired: it

1 **made sense** もっともだ
3 **home** 老人ホーム **destitute** 貧乏な 4 **take on** 引き受ける
5 **resident** このホームの入居者 6 **I'd already been struck** すでに強い印象を受けていた（とても気になっていた） **the way he had of saying "they" or "the others"** 彼が「あの人たち」とか「あの連中」ということ 7 **less often** それほど頻繁にではないが 8 **patients** ホームの入居者 10 **to a certain extent** ある程度 11 **authority** 権威
13 **above the skylight** 天窓の上に 19 **I felt like having a smoke** タバコを吸いたくなった 21 **right there** すぐそこに
24 **At one point** しばらくして 25 **customary** しきたり
28 **drowsy** 眠い 29 **That was how they'd been wired** そんなふうに配線されていた

was all or nothing. I didn't pay too much attention to him after that. He left, came back, set up some chairs. On one of them he stacked some cups around a coffee pot. Then he sat down across from me, on the other side of Maman. The nurse was on that side of the room too, but with her back to me. I couldn't see what she was doing. But the way her arms were moving made me think she was knitting. It was pleasant; the coffee had warmed me up, and the smell of flowers on the night air was coming through the open door. I think I dozed off for a while.

It was a rustling sound that woke me up. Because I'd had my eyes closed, the whiteness of the room seemed even brighter than before. There wasn't a shadow anywhere in front of me, and every object, every angle and curve stood out so sharply it made my eyes hurt. That's when Maman's friends came in. There were about ten in all, and they floated into the blinding light without a sound. They sat down without a single chair creaking. I saw them more clearly than I had ever seen anyone, and not one detail of their faces or their clothes escaped me. But I couldn't hear them, and it was hard for me to believe they really existed. Almost all the women were wearing aprons, and the strings, which were tied tight around their waists, made their bulging stomachs stick out even more. I'd never noticed what huge stomachs old women can have. Almost all the men were skinny and carried canes. What struck me most about their faces was that I couldn't see their eyes, just a faint

1 **all or nothing** 電気をすべてつけるか、すべて消すか 2 **set up** 置いた 3 **stacked** 重ねて置いた 4 **across from me** わたしのむかいに **on the other side of Maman** 母親の横に 6 **with her back to me** 背中を私のほうに向けて 10 **dozed off** 居眠りをした

12 **rustling sound** 何かがすれる音 16 **stood out** 際立っていた 18 **floated** ゆっくり歩いてきた **blinding light** まぶしい光 19 **without a single chair creaking** きしむ音をたてた椅子はひとつもなかった 21 **not one detail of their faces or their clothes escaped me** 彼らの顔も着ているものもすべて細かくみた 24 **aprons** エプロン **strings** 紐 25 **bulging stomachs** せり出たお腹 **stick out** 突きだす 27 **skinny** とてもやせている 28 **carried canes** 杖を持っている **struck** 驚かせた

glimmer in a nest of wrinkles. When they'd sat down, most of them looked at me and nodded awkwardly, their lips sucked in by their toothless mouths, so that I couldn't tell if they were greeting me or if it was just a nervous tic. I think they were greeting me. It was then that I realized they were all sitting across from me, nodding their heads, grouped around the caretaker. For a second I had the ridiculous feeling that they were there to judge me.

Soon one of the women started crying. She was in the second row, hidden behind one of her companions, and I couldn't see her very well. She was crying softly, steadily, in little sobs. I thought she'd never stop. The others seemed not to hear her. They sat there hunched up, gloomy and silent. They would look at the casket, or their canes, or whatever else, but that was all they would look at. The woman kept on crying. It surprised me, because I didn't know who she was. I wished I didn't have to listen to her anymore. But I didn't dare say anything. The caretaker leaned over and said something to her, but she shook her head, mumbled something, and went on crying as much as before. Then the caretaker came around to my side. He sat down next to me. After a long pause he explained, without looking at me, "She was very close to your mother. She says your mother was her only friend and now she hasn't got anyone."

We just sat there like that for quite a while. The woman's sighs and sobs were quieting down. She sniffled a lot. Then finally she shut up. I didn't feel drowsy

1 **glimmer** 輝き、光 **in a nest of wrinkles** シワに隠れて 2 **awkwardly** ぎこちなく 3 **sucked in** すぼめた **I couldn't tell** 私にはわからなかった 4 **greeting** あいさつをしている **nervous tic** 顔の引きつり 7 **grouped** 集まっていた 8 **I had the ridiculous feeling** 私は（that 以下のような）奇妙な感じがした 9 **judge** さばく

11 **row** 列 12 **crying softly, steadily** 声を立てないで、泣き続けていた 13 **sobs** すすり泣き 14 **hunched up** 身を縮めていた 16 **canes** 杖 20 **leaned over** 体をかがめて 21 **mumbled** 小声でいった 26 **now she hasn't got anyone** 彼女にはもうだれもいない

27 **for quite a while** かなりの間 28 **sniffled** 鼻をすする

anymore, but I was tired and my back was hurting me. Now it was all these people not making a sound that was getting on my nerves. Except that every now and then I'd hear a strange noise and I couldn't figure out what it was. Finally I realized that some of the old people were sucking at the insides of their cheeks and making these weird smacking noises. They were so lost in their thoughts that they weren't even aware of it. I even had the impression that the dead woman lying in front of them didn't mean anything to them. But I think now that that was a false impression.

We all had some coffee, served by the caretaker. After that I don't know any more. The night passed. I remember opening my eyes at one point and seeing that all the old people were slumped over asleep, except for one old man, with his chin resting on the back of his hands wrapped around his cane, who was staring at me as if he were just waiting for me to wake up. Then I dozed off again. I woke up because my back was hurting more and more. Dawn was creeping up over the skylight. Soon afterwards, one of the old men woke up and coughed a lot. He kept hacking into a large checkered handkerchief, and every cough was like a convulsion. He woke the others up, and the caretaker told them that they ought to be going. They got up. The uncomfortable vigil had left their faces ashen looking. On their way out, and much to my surprise, they all shook my hand—as if that night during which we hadn't exchanged as much as a single word had somehow brought us closer together.

1 **my back** 私の背中　2 **was getting on my nerves** 私をいらいらさせていた（ここも it was...that の強調構文）　3 **every now and then** ときどき　6 **sucking at the insides of their cheeks** 頬の内側を吸っている　7 **smacking noises** ピチャピチャいう音　**lost in their thoughts** 物思いにふけっていた　11 **a false impression**　間違った印象（考え）
15 **slumped over asleep** 眠ってだらしない格好をしていた　16 **with his chin resting on the back of his hands wrapped around his cane** あごを、杖を握った両手の甲にのせている　18 **dozed off** 居眠りをしてしまった　20 **Dawn** 朝日　22 **hacking** 咳をしている　**checkered** 格子縞の　23 **convulsion** 痙攣　**woke the others up** ほかの人たちを起こした　25 **be going** 葬儀にいく　26 **ashen** 青白い　27 **much to my surprise** 私がとても驚いたことに　**that night...had somehow brought us closer together**（had の主語は that night で、during から word までが that night を修飾している）私たちがひとことも交わさなかったこの夜が、なんとなく私たちを親密にしてくれた

I was tired. The caretaker took me to his room and I was able to clean up a little. I had some more coffee and milk, which was very good. When I went outside, the sun was up. Above the hills that separate Marengo from the sea, the sky was streaked with red. And the wind coming over the hills brought the smell of salt with it. It was going to be a beautiful day. It had been a long time since I'd been out in the country, and I could feel how much I'd enjoy going for a walk if it hadn't been for Maman.

But I waited in the courtyard, under a plane tree. I breathed in the smell of fresh earth and I wasn't sleepy anymore. I thought of the other guys at the office. They'd be getting up to go to work about this time: for me that was always the most difficult time of day. I thought about those things a little more, but I was distracted by the sound of a bell ringing inside the buildings. There was some commotion behind the windows, then everything quieted down again. The sun was now a little higher in the sky: it was starting to warm my feet. The caretaker came across the courtyard and told me that the director was asking for me. I went to his office. He had me sign a number of documents. I noticed that he was dressed in black with pin-striped trousers. He picked up the telephone and turned to me. "The undertaker's men arrived a few minutes ago. I'm going to ask them to seal the casket. Before I do, would you like to see your mother one last time?" I said no. He gave the order into the telephone, lowering his voice: "Figeac,

2 **clean up** 身なりを整える（髪をとかしたり、顔を洗ったり） 4 **the hills that separate Marengo from the sea** マランゴを海から隔てている丘　6 **streaked with red** 赤い筋が走っている 7 **out in the country** こんな田舎に　10 **if it hadn't been for Maman**（仮定法）母親の件がなかったら
11 **plane** スズカケノキ、プラタナス　16 **was distracted** 気が散った　18 **commotion** 騒々しい音　23 **had me sign** 私に署名させた　24 **pin-striped** 細い縦縞の　25 **undertaker's** 葬儀屋の 27 **seal the casket** 棺のふたを閉めてしまう　29 **Figeac** フィジャック（電話で話している相手の名前）

tell the men they can go ahead."

After that he told me he would be attending the funeral and I thanked him. He sat down behind his desk and crossed his short legs. He informed me that he and I would be the only ones there, apart from the nurse on duty. The residents usually weren't allowed to attend funerals. He only let them keep the vigil. "It's more humane that way," he remarked. But in this case he'd given one of mother's old friends—Thomas Pérez—permission to join the funeral procession. At that the director smiled. He said, "I'm sure you understand. It's a rather childish sentiment. But he and your mother were almost inseparable. The others used to tease them and say, 'Pérez has a fiancée.' He'd laugh. They enjoyed it. And the truth is he's taking Madame Meursault's death very hard. I didn't think I could rightfully refuse him permission. But on the advice of our visiting physician, I did not allow him to keep the vigil last night."

We didn't say anything for quite a long time. The director stood up and looked out the window of his office. A moment later he said, "Here's the priest from Marengo already. He's early." He warned me that it would take at least three-quarters of an hour to walk to the church, which is in the village itself. We went downstairs. Out in front of the building stood the priest and two altar boys. One of them was holding a censer, and the priest was leaning toward him, adjusting the length of its silver chain. As we approached, the priest straightened up. He called me "my son" and said a few words to me. He

1 **the men** みんな　5 **apart from the nurse** 看護師を別にすれば　6 **residents** ホームの入居者　10 **procession** 行列、行進 **At that** その点に関して、そのことで　12 **rather** とても　13 **inseparable** 引き離すことができない　**tease** からかう　16 **hard** つらい　**refuse him permission** 彼に許可を与えない　17 **visiting physician** 往診の医師

24 **Out in front of the building** 建物の前に　25 **altar boys** 祭壇奉仕者の役を行う少年　26 **censer** 吊り香炉　28 **straightened up** 背筋をのばした

went inside; I followed.

I noticed right away that the screws on the casket had been tightened and that there were four men wearing black in the room. The director was telling me that the hearse was waiting out in the road and at the same time I could hear the priest beginning his prayers. From then on everything happened very quickly. The men moved toward the casket with a pall. The priest, his acolytes, the director and I all went outside. A woman I didn't know was standing by the door. "Monsieur Meursault," the director said. I didn't catch the woman's name; I just understood that she was the nurse assigned by the home. Without smiling she lowered her long, gaunt face. Then we stepped aside to make way for the body. We followed the pall bearers and left the home. Outside the gate stood the hearse. Varnished, glossy, and oblong, it reminded me of a pencil box. Next to it was the funeral director, a little man in a ridiculous getup, and an awkward, embarrassed-looking old man. I realized that it was Monsieur Pérez. He was wearing a soft felt hat with a round crown and a wide brim (he took it off as the casket was coming through the gate), a suit with trousers that were corkscrewed down around his ankles, and a black tie with a knot that was too small for the big white collar of his shirt. His lips were trembling below a nose dotted with blackheads. Strange, floppy, thick-rimmed ears stuck out through his fine, white hair, and I was struck by their blood-red color next to the pallor of his face. The funeral director assigned us our places.

2 **the screws** ねじ釘 5 **hearse** 霊柩車（ここでは、おそらく棺を運ぶ馬車） **out in the road** 道で 6 **From then on** それからは 8 **a pall** 棺にかける布 **acolytes** 司祭の助手 12 **assigned by the home** このホームに雇われている 13 **gaunt** 頬のこけた 14 **stepped aside** わきにどいた **make way for the body** 遺体に道をあける 15 **pall bearers** 棺を運ぶ人たち 16 **Varnished** ニスを塗った **glossy** 光沢のある **oblong** 長方形の 18 **a ridiculous getup** 間の抜けた服装 19 **awkward** ぎこちない **embarrassed-looking** 不安そうな表情の 20 **felt hat** フェルトの帽子 21 **a round crown** 上の部分が丸い **wide brim** つば広の 23 **corkscrewed** ねじれていた 24 **knot** 結び目 26 **dotted with blackheads** 黒ずんだ毛穴がぽつぽつと目立っている **floppy** たれている **thick-rimmed** 縁が厚い 27 **stuck out** 突き出ていた **fine, white hair** 細い白髪 28 **pallor** 青白さ

First came the priest, then the hearse. Flanking it, the four men. Behind it, the director and myself and, bringing up the rear, the nurse and Monsieur Pérez.

The sky was already filled with light. The sun was beginning to bear down on the earth and it was getting hotter by the minute. I don't know why we waited so long before getting under way. I was hot in my dark clothes. The little old man, who had put his hat back on, took it off again. I turned a little in his direction and was looking at him when the director started talking to me about him. He told me that my mother and Monsieur Pérez often used to walk down to the village together in the evenings, accompanied by a nurse. I was looking at the countryside around me. Seeing the rows of cypress trees leading up to the hills next to the sky, and the houses standing out here and there against that red and green earth, I was able to understand Maman better. Evenings in that part of the country must have been a kind of sad relief. But today, with the sun bearing down, making the whole landscape shimmer with heat, it was inhuman and oppressive.

We got under way. It was then that I noticed that Pérez had a slight limp. Little by little, the hearse was picking up speed and the old man was losing ground. One of the men flanking the hearse had also dropped back and was now even with me. I was surprised at how fast the sun was climbing in the sky. I noticed that for quite some time the countryside had been buzzing with the sound of insects and the crackling of grass. The sweat

1 **Flanking** 側面に立っている 2 **bringing up the rear** 最後についている

5 **bear down on the earth** 大地に激しく照りつける 6 **by the minute** 1分ごとに 7 **getting under way** 出発する 14 **countryside** 田舎、地方 15 **cypress** イトスギ **next to the sky** 空に接している 16 **against** ～を背景に 19 **sad relief** 寂しい休息 20 **shimmer** 揺らめく 21 **inhuman and oppressive** 非人間的で窮屈な

23 **a slight limp** 少し足を引きずっていること 24 **was losing ground** 遅れていった 25 **dropped back** 遅れた 26 **even with me** 私の横に並ぶ 29 **insects** 虫 **crackling of grass** ざわざわという葉ずれの音

was pouring down my face. I wasn't wearing a hat, so I fanned myself with my handkerchief. The man from the undertaker's said something to me then which I missed. He was lifting the edge of his cap with his right hand and wiping his head with a handkerchief with his left at the same time. I said, "What?" He pointed up at the sky and repeated, "Pretty hot." I said, "Yes." A minute later he asked, "Is that your mother in there?" Again I said, "Yes." "Was she old?" I answered, "Fairly," because I didn't know the exact number. After that he was quiet. I turned around and saw old Pérez about fifty meters behind us. He was going as fast as he could, swinging his felt hat at the end of his arm. I looked at the director, too. He was walking with great dignity, without a single wasted motion. A few beads of sweat were forming on his forehead, but he didn't wipe them off.

The procession seemed to me to be moving a little faster. All around me there was still the same glowing countryside flooded with sunlight. The glare from the sky was unbearable. At one point, we went over a section of the road that had just been repaved. The tar had burst open in the sun. Our feet sank into it, leaving its shiny pulp exposed. Sticking up above the top of the hearse, the coachman's hard leather hat looked as if it had been molded out of the same black mud. I felt a little lost between the blue and white of the sky and the monotony of the colors around me—the sticky black of the tar, the dull black of all the clothes, and the shiny black of the hearse. All of it—the sun, the smell

2 **The man from the undertaker's** 葬儀屋の男　3 **missed** 聞き逃した　8 **that** 遺骸のこと　9 **Fairly** かなり　10 **the exact number** 正確な数（年齢）　13 **at the end of his arm** 腕の先で（手に持って）　14 **with great dignity** とても堂々と　**without a single wasted motion** 無駄な動きなどまったくなく　15 **beads** 粒　16 **forehead** 額
19 **flooded with sunlight** 日の光であふれた　21 **repaved** 舗装し直された　**tar had burst open** タールが溶けていた　23 **shiny pulp** ぎらぎらしたねばつくもの（タール）　**top** 上　24 **coachman's** 御者の　25 **molded out of the same black mud** この黒い泥（タール）を型に流しこんで作った　26 **lost** ぼんやりする　27 **monotony** 単調さ　**sticky** ねばっこい　28 **dull** 鈍い

of leather and horse dung from the hearse, the smell of varnish and incense, and my fatigue after a night without sleep—was making it hard for me to see or think straight. I turned around again: Pérez seemed to be way back there, fading in the shimmering heat. Then I lost sight of him altogether. I looked around and saw that he'd left the road and cut out across the fields. I also noticed there was a bend in the road up ahead. I realized that Pérez, who knew the country, was taking a short cut in order to catch up with us. By the time we rounded the bend, he was back with us. Then we lost him again. He set off cross country once more, and so it went on. I could feel the blood pounding in my temples.

After that, everything seemed to happen so fast, so deliberately, so naturally that I don't remember any of it anymore. Except for one thing: as we entered the village, the nurse spoke to me. She had a remarkable voice which didn't go with her face at all, a melodious, quavering voice. She said, "If you go slowly, you risk getting sunstroke. But if you go too fast, you work up a sweat and then catch a chill inside the church." She was right. There was no way out. Several other images from that day have stuck in my mind: for instance, Pérez's face when he caught up with us for the last time, just outside the village. Big tears of frustration and exhaustion were streaming down his cheeks. But because of all the wrinkles, they weren't dripping off. They spread out and ran together again, leaving a watery film over his ruined face. Then there was the church and the

1 **dung** 糞 2 **varnish** ニス **incense** 香 **fatigue** 疲れ 3 **think straight** ちゃんと考える 5 **fading** 消えかかる 7 **cut out across the fields** 畑を横切る 8 **bend** カーブ **up ahead** 前方に 9 **short cut** 近道 10 **catch up with** 追いつく 12 **so it went on** それがくり返された 13 **the blood pounding in my temples** こめかみで血液が脈打っている

15 **deliberately** 着々と 16 **Except for one thing** ひとつだけ例外があった 17 **remarkable** 変わった 18 **go with** 似合う 19 **quavering** 震えるような 20 **sunstroke** 熱射病 **work up a sweat** 汗をかく 21 **catch a chill** 悪寒がする 22 **no way out** どうしようもない状態 23 **stuck in my mind** 頭にこびりついている 25 **frustration** 苦痛 **exhaustion** 疲労 26 **because of all the wrinkles** たくさんのシワのせいで 28 **watery film** 水の膜 29 **ruined face** 荒れ放題の顔

villagers on the sidewalks, the red geraniums on the graves in the cemetery, Pérez fainting (he crumpled like a rag doll), the blood-red earth spilling over Maman's casket, the white flesh of the roots mixed in with it, more people, voices, the village, waiting in front of a café, the incessant drone of the motor, and my joy when the bus entered the nest of lights that was Algiers and I knew I was going to go to bed and sleep for twelve hours.

1 **geraniums** ゼラニウム　2 **cemetery** 墓地　**fainting** 気を失っている　**crumpled** へたってしまった。ぐったり倒れこんだ　3 **rag doll** 布で作った人形　4 **the white flesh of the roots** 根の白い部分　**mixed in with it** それ（土）に混じった　6 **incessant drone** 絶え間ないうなり　7 **nest of lights** 光の巣

2

As I was waking up, it came to me why my boss had seemed annoyed when I asked him for two days off: today is Saturday. I'd sort of forgotten, but as I was getting up, it came to me. And, naturally, my boss thought about the fact that I'd be getting four days' vacation that way, including Sunday, and he couldn't have been happy about that. But, in the first place, it isn't my fault if they buried Maman yesterday instead of today, and second, I would have had Saturday and Sunday off anyway. Obviously, that still doesn't keep me from understanding my boss's point of view.

I had a hard time getting up, because I was tired from the day before. While I was shaving, I wondered what I was going to do and I decided to go for a swim. I caught the streetcar to go to the public beach down at the harbor. Once there, I dove into the channel. There were lots of young people. In the water I ran into Marie Cardona, a former typist in our office whom I'd had a thing for at the time. She did too, I think. But she'd left soon afterwards and we didn't have the time. I helped her onto a float and as I did, I brushed against her breasts. I was still in the water when she was already lying flat on her stomach on the float. She turned toward me. Her hair was in her eyes and she was laughing. I hoisted myself up next to her. It was nice, and, sort of joking around, I let my head fall back and rest on her stomach. She didn't say anything so I left it there. I had the whole sky

3 **it came to me** it（why 以下のこと）がわかった　4 **annoyed** 不機嫌な　5 **sort of**（婉曲表現）ちょっと、なんとなく
12 **keep me from understanding** 私が理解することを妨げる
13 **point of view** 考え
14 **I had a hard time getting up** 起きるのがつらかった
17 **streetcar** 電車　18 **channel** 湾　19 **ran into** ばったり出くわす　**Marie Cardona** マリー・カルドナ　20 **had a thing for** 好きだった　21 **at the time** その頃　23 **float**（海に浮いている）ブイ　**brushed** こする、触れる　24 **on her stomach** 腹ばいに
26 **hoisted myself up**（ブイの）上にあがる　27 **, sort of joking around,**（挿入句）冗談めかして　29 **I left it there** 私は頭をそのままにしていた

in my eyes and it was blue and gold. On the back of my neck I could feel Marie's heart beating softly. We lay on the float for a long time, half asleep. When the sun got too hot, she dove off and I followed. I caught up with her, put my arm around her waist, and we swam together. She laughed the whole time. On the dock, while we were drying ourselves off, she said, "I'm darker than you." I asked her if she wanted to go to the movies that evening. She laughed again and told me there was a Fernandel movie she'd like to see. Once we were dressed, she seemed very surprised to see I was wearing a black tie and she asked me if I was in mourning. I told her Maman had died. She wanted to know how long ago, so I said, "Yesterday." She gave a little start but didn't say anything. I felt like telling her it wasn't my fault, but I stopped myself because I remembered that I'd already said that to my boss. It didn't mean anything. Besides, you always feel a little guilty.

By that evening Marie had forgotten all about it. The movie was funny in parts, but otherwise it was just too stupid. She had her leg pressed against mine. I was fondling her breasts. Toward the end of the show, I gave her a kiss, but not a good one. She came back to my place.

When I woke up, Marie had gone. She'd explained to me that she had to go to her aunt's. I remembered that it was Sunday, and that bothered me: I don't like Sundays. So I rolled over, tried to find the salty smell Marie's hair had left on the pillow, and slept until ten. Then I smoked a few cigarettes, still in bed, till noon. I didn't feel like

6 **dock** ドック、埠頭　9 **Fernandel movie** フェルナンデル（喜劇俳優、シャンソン歌手）の出ている映画　12 **in mourning** 喪に服している、喪中　14 **start** 驚き（の表情、声）　18 **you**（一般人称）

21 **mine** my leg　**fondling** もてあそぶ　22 **the show** 映画

23 **She came back to my place** 私の部屋にやってきた

27 **rolled over** ごろっと転がる　**salty smell** 潮の香

having lunch at Céleste's like I usually did because they'd be sure to ask questions and I don't like that. I fixed myself some eggs and ate them out of the pan, without bread because I didn't have any left and I didn't feel like going downstairs to buy some.

After lunch I was a little bored and I wandered around the apartment. It was just the right size when Maman was here. Now it's too big for me, and I've had to move the dining room table into my bedroom. I live in just one room now, with some saggy straw chairs, a wardrobe whose mirror has gone yellow, a dressing table, and a brass bed. I've let the rest go. A little later, just for something to do, I picked up an old newspaper and read it. I cut out an advertisement for Kruschen Salts and stuck it in an old notebook where I put things from the papers that interest me. I also washed my hands, and then I went out onto the balcony.

My room looks out over the main street in the neighborhood. It was a beautiful afternoon. Yet the pavement was wet and slippery, and what few people there were were in a hurry. First, it was families out for a walk: two little boys in sailor suits, with trousers below the knees, looking a little cramped in their stiff clothes, and a little girl with a big pink bow and black patent-leather shoes. Behind them, an enormous mother, in a brown silk dress, and the father, a rather frail little man I know by sight. He had on a straw hat and a bow tie and was carrying a walking stick. Seeing him with his wife, I understood why people in the neighborhood said he was

3 **fixed myself some eggs** 自分で卵を焼いた **out of the pan** フライパンからそのまま 5 **some** some bread
10 **saggy** 座面がへこんだ **straw chairs** 麦ワラを編んで作った椅子 **wardrobe** ワードローブ 11 **dressing table** 鏡台
12 **brass** 真鍮 **let the rest go** そのほかのものはどうでもいい
14 **advertisement** 広告 **Kruschen Salts** クルッシェンの塩（イギリス製の入浴剤）
18 **looks out** 見下ろす 19 **Yet** しかし 20 **what few people there were** そこにいるほんの少しの人たち 22 **sailor suits** セーラー服 **trousers below the knees** 膝下までのズボン
23 **cramped** 体がこわばっている **stiff clothes** 窮屈そうな服 24 **bow** リボン **patent-leather** エナメル 26 **frail** やせた **I know by sight** 見かけたことのある 27 **bow tie** 蝶ネクタイ

distinguished. A little later the local boys went by, hair greased back, red ties, tight-fitting jackets, with embroidered pocket handkerchiefs and square-toed shoes. I thought they must be heading to the movies in town. That was why they were leaving so early and hurrying toward the streetcar, laughing loudly.

After them, the street slowly emptied out. The matinees had all started, I guess. The only ones left were the shopkeepers and the cats. The sky was clear but dull above the fig trees lining the street. On the sidewalk across the way the tobacconist brought out a chair, set it in front of his door, and straddled it, resting his arms on the back. The streetcars, packed a few minutes before, were almost empty. In the little café Chez Pierrot, next door to the tobacconist's, the waiter was sweeping up the sawdust in the deserted restaurant inside. It was Sunday all right.

I turned my chair around and set it down like the tobacconist's because I found that it was more comfortable that way. I smoked a couple of cigarettes, went inside to get a piece of chocolate, and went back to the window to eat it. Soon after that, the sky grew dark and I thought we were in for a summer storm. Gradually, though, it cleared up again. But the passing clouds had left a hint of rain hanging over the street, which made it look darker. I sat there for a long time and watched the sky.

At five o'clock some streetcars pulled up, clanging away. They were bringing back gangs of fans from the

1 **distinguished** 上品な、品のある　**local** 土地の　2 **greased back** 油を塗って後ろになでつけた　**embroidered** 刺繍をした
3 **square-toed shoes** つま先の四角い靴
7 **emptied out** ひと気がなくなった　**matinees** マチネ（芝居などの昼の公演）　9 **dull** 鈍い色　10 **fig** イチジク　**lining the street** 道沿いに並んでいる　11 **tobacconist** タバコ屋　12 **straddled** またぐように座った　13 **packed**（人で）混んでいた　14 **Chez Pierrot** ピエロ亭（カフェの名前）　15 **sweeping up** せっせと掃除をしていた　16 **sawdust** おがくず（バーやカフェなどで、昔、よく床にまいていた。飲み物や食べ物が床にこぼれても、すべらないし、細かいごみを吸着してくれる）　**deserted** 客のいない　17 **all right** 申し分ない
18 **set it down** 置いた　23 **in for** ～に直面する　24 **passing clouds** 流れていく雲　25 **left a hint of rain hanging over the street** かすかな雨を路上に残していった
28 **pulled up** 到着した　**clanging away** ガチャンと音をたてて
29 **gangs of fans** 大勢の観客

local soccer stadium. They were crowded onto the running boards and hanging from the handrails. The streetcars that followed brought back the players, whom I recognized by their little athletic bags. They were shouting and singing at the tops of their lungs that their team would never die. Several of them waved to me. One of them even yelled up to me, "We beat 'em!" And I nodded, as if to say "Yes." From then on there was a steady stream of cars.

The sky changed again. Above the rooftops the sky had taken on a reddish glow, and with evening coming on the streets came to life. People were straggling back from their walks. I recognized the distinguished little man among the others. Children were either crying or lagging behind. Almost all at once moviegoers spilled out of the neighborhood theaters into the street. The young men among them were gesturing more excitedly than usual and I thought they must have seen an adventure film. The ones who had gone to the movies in town came back a little later. They looked more serious. They were still laughing, but only now and then, and they seemed tired and dreamy. But they hung around anyway, walking up and down the sidewalk across the street. The local girls, bareheaded, were walking arm in arm. The young men had made sure they would have to bump right into them and then they would make cracks. The girls giggled and turned their heads away. Several of the girls, whom I knew, waved to me.

Then the street lamps came on all of a sudden and

1 **running boards** 電車の乗降口のステップ　2 **handrails** 手すり　4 **recognized by their little athletic bags** 小さなスポーツバッグで（選手だと）わかった　5 **at the tops of their lungs** 声の限りに　7 **yelled up** 大声で叫ぶ　**We beat 'em!** おれたちが勝った！　8 **From then on** その頃から

12 **came to life** 活気づいてきた　**straggling** のんびり歩く　15 **lagging behind** ぐずぐず後ろを歩いている　**moviegoers spilled out of** 映画好きの人たちがあふれ出てきた　19 **adventure film** 冒険映画　20 **serious** まじめな　21 **now and then** ときどき　22 **hung around** ぶらぶらする　24 **bareheaded** 帽子をかぶっていない　26 **bump right into them** 彼女たちにまともにぶつかる　**make cracks** ひやかす　27 **giggled** くすくす笑った　**turned their heads away** 顔をそむけた

29 **all of a sudden** いきなり

made the first stars appearing in the night sky grow dim. I felt my eyes getting tired from watching the street filled with so many people and lights. The street lamps were making the pavement glisten, and the light from the streetcars would glint off someone's shiny hair, or off a smile or a silver bracelet. Soon afterwards, with the streetcars running less often and the sky already blue above the trees and the lamps, the neighborhood emptied out, almost imperceptibly, until the first cat slowly made its way across the now deserted street. Then I thought maybe I ought to have some dinner. My neck was a little stiff from resting my chin on the back of the chair for so long. I went downstairs to buy some bread and spaghetti, did my cooking, and ate standing up. I wanted to smoke a cigarette at the window, but the air was getting colder and I felt a little chilled. I shut my windows, and as I was coming back I glanced at the mirror and saw a corner of my table with my alcohol lamp next to some pieces of bread. It occurred to me that anyway one more Sunday was over, that Maman was buried now, that I was going back to work, and that, really, nothing had changed.

1 **made the first stars appearing in the night sky grow dim** 夜空に現れた最初の星々の光を鈍くした　5 **glint off** 輝かせる　9 **imperceptibly** 知らず知らずのうちに　10 **made its way** 進む、歩く　12 **from resting my chin on the back of the chair for so long**（from は理由、原因を表す）あごを椅子の背の上に長いこと置いていたために　16 **felt a little chilled** ちょっと寒かった　19 **It occurred to me that** that 以下のことが頭に浮かんだ（that は 4 つある。① that anyway...　② that Maman...　③ that I...　④ that, really...)

3

I worked hard at the office today. The boss was nice. He asked me if I wasn't too tired and he also wanted to know Maman's age. I said, "About sixty," so as not to make a mistake; and I don't know why, but he seemed to be relieved somehow and to consider the matter closed.

There was a stack of freight invoices that had piled up on my desk, and I had to go through them all. Before leaving the office to go to lunch, I washed my hands. I really like doing this at lunchtime. I don't enjoy it so much in the evening, because the roller towel you use is soaked through: one towel has to last all day. I mentioned it once to my boss. He told me he was sorry but it was really a minor detail. I left a little late, at half past twelve, with Emmanuel, who works as a dispatcher. The office overlooks the sea, and we took a minute to watch the freighters in the harbor, which was ablaze with sunlight. Then a truck came toward us with its chains rattling and its engine backfiring. Emmanuel said, "How 'bout it?" and I started running. The truck passed us and we ran after it. I was engulfed by the noise and the dust. I couldn't see anything, and all I was conscious of was the sensation of hurtling forward in a mad dash through cranes and winches, masts bobbing on the horizon and the hulls of ships alongside us as we ran. I was first to grab hold and take a flying leap. Then I reached out and helped Emmanuel scramble up. We were out of breath;

3 **nice** 機嫌がいい　5 **so as not to make a mistake** 間違った答えをしないように　7 **the matter closed** この件は終わった　9 **stack** 積み重なっている状態　**freight invoices** 船荷の送り状　10 **go through**　目を通す、チェックする　13 **the roller towel** 両端を縫い合わせて輪にした回転式のタオル　14 **soaked** 濡れている　**through** 完全に　**one towel has to last all day** 1枚のタオルを一日中使うようになっている　16 **a minor detail** どうでもいい細かいこと　17 **Emmanuel** エマニュエル　**dispatcher** 発送係　18 **took a minute** 1分ほど〜した　19 **freighters** 貨物船　**ablaze** ぎらぎら輝いている　21 **backfiring** 逆火を起こしている　**How ’bout it?** あれをやるか？　23 **was engulfed** 包まれた　24 **all I was conscious of** 私が意識していたのは〜だけだった　25 **the sensation of hurtling forward** 前に突っ走る快感　**mad dash** 全力疾走　26 **cranes**　クレーン、起重機　**winches** ウインチ、巻き上げ機　**masts bobbing on the horizon** 水平線の上で上下しているマスト　27 **the hulls of ships** 船体　**alongside us** 私たちの横の　28 **grab hold** つかまる（何につかまるのかは書かれていないがp62の最初の行にthe truckとあるので、おそらくトラックの荷台）　**flying leap** 飛びあがること　**reached out** 手をのばした　29 **scramble up** よじ登った　**out of breath** 息が切れる

the truck was bumping around on the uneven cobblestones of the quay in a cloud of dust and sun. Emmanuel was laughing so hard he could hardly breathe.

We arrived at Céleste's dripping with sweat. Céleste was there, as always, with his big belly, his apron, and his white moustache. He asked me if things were "all right now." I told him yes they were and said I was hungry. I ate fast and had some coffee. Then I went home and slept for a while because I'd drunk too much wine, and when I woke up I felt like having a smoke. It was late and I ran to catch a streetcar. I worked all afternoon. It got very hot in the office, and that evening, when I left, I was glad to walk back slowly along the docks. The sky was green; I felt good. But I went straight home because I wanted to boil myself some potatoes.

On my way upstairs, in the dark, I ran into old Salamano, my neighbor across the landing. He was with his dog. The two of them have been inseparable for eight years. The spaniel has a skin disease—mange, I think—which makes almost all its hair fall out and leaves it covered with brown sores and scabs. After living together for so long, the two of them alone in one tiny room, they've ended up looking like each other. Old Salamano has reddish scabs on his face and wispy yellow hair. As for the dog, he's sort of taken on his master's stooped look, muzzle down, neck straining. They look as if they belong to the same species, and yet they hate each other. Twice a day, at eleven and six, the old man takes the dog out for a walk. They haven't changed their route in

1 **bumping** 大きく揺れる **uneven** ふぞろいな **cobblestones** 丸石 2 **quay** 埠頭、波止場 **a cloud of dust** 土埃
4 **dripping with sweat** 汗をたらしながら 5 **belly** 腹
6 **moustache** 口ひげ **things were "all right now"**（物事が）うまくいっている 7 **yes they were** yes, things were "all right now" 13 **docks** ドック、波止場
16 **On my way upstairs** アパートの階段を上がっていく途中で **old Salamano** サラマノじいさん 17 **across the landing** 踊り場で 19 **spaniel** スパニエル犬 **mange** 疥癬（寄生虫による伝染性の皮膚病） 21 **sores** ただれ **scabs** かさぶた 22 **the two of them alone** サラマノじいさんと犬だけで 23 **ended up** そのうち〜になった **looking like each other** お互いに似ている 24 **wispy** わずかの 25 **taken on** 〜を受け継いでいる **stooped look** 前かがみの姿勢 26 **muzzle down** うつむいた姿勢 **neck straining** 首を伸ばした姿勢 27 **belong to the same species** 同じ種に属している **and yet** しかし、そのくせ

eight years. You can see them in the rue de Lyon, the dog pulling the man along until old Salamano stumbles. Then he beats the dog and swears at it. The dog cowers and trails behind. Then it's the old man who pulls the dog. Once the dog has forgotten, it starts dragging its master along again, and again gets beaten and sworn at. Then they both stand there on the sidewalk and stare at each other, the dog in terror, the man in hatred. It's the same thing every day. When the dog wants to urinate, the old man won't give him enough time and yanks at him, so that the spaniel leaves behind a trail of little drops. If the dog has an accident in the room, it gets beaten again. This has been going on for eight years. Céleste is always saying, "It's pitiful," but really, who's to say? When I ran into him on the stairs, Salamano was swearing away at the dog. He was saying, "Filthy, stinking bastard!" and the dog was whimpering. I said "Good evening," but the old man just went on cursing. So I asked him what the dog had done. He didn't answer. All he said was "Filthy, stinking bastard!" I could barely see him leaning over his dog, trying to fix something on its collar. I spoke louder. Then, without turning around, he answered with a kind of suppressed rage, "He's always there." Then he left, yanking at the animal, which was letting itself be dragged along, whimpering.

Just then my other neighbor came in. The word around the neighborhood is that he lives off women. But when you ask him what he does, he's a "warehouse guard." Generally speaking, he's not very popular. But

1 **the rue de Lyon** リヨン通り 2 **stumbles** よろめく 3 **swears** ののしる **cowers** 小さくなる 4 **trails behind** 後ろをついていく 6 **gets beaten and sworn at** なぐられ、ののしられる 9 **urinate** 小便をする 10 **yanks**（リードを）ぐいと引く 11 **a trail of little drops** 小さな（小便の）滴のあと 12 **accident** おもらし 14 **who's to say?** だれにわかるだろうか 16 **swearing away** 激しくののしる **Filthy** 不潔な、きたならしい **stinking bastard!** くさいやつ！ 17 **whimpering** くんくん鳴いている 18 **went on cursing** ののしり続けていた 21 **leaning over** かがみこんでいる **fix something on its collar** 首輪のどこかを直す 23 **suppressed rage** 抑えた怒り 24 **which was letting itself be dragged along**（which の先行詞は the animal、つまり犬）引きずられるがままになっていた
26 **The word around the neighborhood** 近所のうわさ
27 **lives off women** 女に寄生して食っている 28 **warehouse guard** 倉庫番 29 **Generally speaking** 一般的な評価によれば **popular** 人気がある

he often talks to me and sometimes stops by my place for a minute, because I listen to him. I find what he has to say interesting. Besides, I don't have any reason not to talk to him. His name is Raymond Sintès. He's a little on the short side, with broad shoulders and a nose like a boxer's. He always dresses very sharp. And once he said to me, talking about Salamano, "If that isn't pitiful!" He asked me didn't I think it was disgusting and I said no.

We went upstairs and I was about to leave him when he said, "I've got some blood sausage and some wine at my place. How about joining me?" I figured it would save me the trouble of having to cook for myself, so I accepted. He has only one room too, and a little kitchen with no window. Over his bed he has a pink-and-white plaster angel, some pictures of famous athletes, and two or three photographs of naked women. The room was dirty and the bed was unmade. First he lit his paraffin lamp, then he took a pretty dubious-looking bandage out of his pocket and wrapped it around his right hand. I asked him what he'd done to it. He said he'd been in a fight with some guy who was trying to start trouble.

"You see, Monsieur Meursault," he said, "it's not that I'm a bad guy, but I have a short fuse. This guy says to me, 'If you're man enough you'll get down off that streetcar.' I said, 'C'mon, take it easy.' Then he said, 'You're yellow.' So I got off and I said to him, 'I think you better stop right there or I'm gonna have to teach you a lesson.' And he said, 'You and who else?' So I let him have it. He went down. I was about to help him up

1 **my place** 私の部屋 2 **I find what he has to say interesting** 私は彼の話すこと（what he has to say）を面白いと思う 4 **Raymond Sintès** レイモン・サンテス **a little on the short side** ちょっと背が低い 6 **sharp** スマートな 7 **If that isn't pitiful!** まったく、かわいそうだ！ 8 **disgusting** むかつく

10 **blood sausage** ブラッドソーセージ（肉に血を混ぜて作ったソーセージ） 11 **joining me**（食事や酒に）つきあう 12 **save me the trouble of having to cook for myself** 食事を作る手間が省ける 15 **plaster** 石膏 **athletes** スポーツ選手 17 **unmade** 整えられていない（シーツなどがしわくちゃのまま） **paraffin lamp** 石油ランプ 18 **dubious-looking** よごれた、きたならしい 20 **what he'd done to it**（it=his right hand）右手をどうしたのか 21 **start trouble** けんかを売る

23 **have a short fuse** 気が短い 24 **man enough** 男らしい男 **get down off that streetcar** 電車から降りる 25 **take it easy** 落ち着け 26 **yellow** 臆病 27 **teach you a lesson** 痛い目に合わせる 28 **You and who else?** そんなおどしは怖くもなんともない **I let him have it** 一発殴ってやった 29 **went down** 倒れた

but he started kicking me from there on the ground. So I kneed him one and slugged him a couple of times. His face was all bloody. I asked him if he'd had enough. He said, 'Yes.' " All this time, Sintès was fiddling with his bandage. I was sitting on the bed. He said, "So you see, I wasn't the one who started it. He was asking for it." It was true and I agreed. Then he told me that as a matter of fact he wanted to ask my advice about the whole business, because I was a man, I knew about things, I could help him out, and then we'd be pals. I didn't say anything, and he asked me again if I wanted to be pals. I said it was fine with me: he seemed pleased. He got out the blood sausage, fried it up, and set out glasses, plates, knives and forks, and two bottles of wine. All this in silence. Then we sat down. As we ate, he started telling me his story. He was a little hesitant at first. "I knew this lady . . . as a matter of fact, well, she was my mistress." The man he'd had the fight with was this woman's brother. He told me he'd been keeping her. I didn't say anything, and yet right away he added that he knew what people around the neighborhood were saying, but that his conscience was clear and that he was a warehouse guard.

"To get back to what I was saying," he continued, "I realized that she was cheating on me." He'd been giving her just enough to live on. He paid the rent on her room and gave her twenty francs a day for food. "Three hundred francs for the room, six hundred for food, a pair of stockings every now and then—that made it a thousand

2 **kneed** 膝でいっぱつくらわした **slugged** こぶしで殴った 4 **fiddling with** 〜をいじっている 7 **as a matter of fact** 実際のところ 8 **whole business** この件全体 9 **knew about things** 物事がわかっている 10 **help him out** 助ける **pals** 仲間 12 **seemed pleased** うれしそうだった 13 **fried it up** こんがり焼いた **set out** 並べた 16 **hesitant** ためらう 18 **my mistress** おれの女 **The man he'd had the fight with** 彼がけんかをした男 19 **keeping** 養っている 20 **right away** すぐに 22 **his conscience was clear** 良心にやましいところはなかった 24 **To get back** 〜にもどる 25 **was cheating on me** おれをだましていた 26 **enough to live on** 食っていくのに十分なもの 27 **francs** フラン（当時のフランスの通貨） 29 **every now and then** ときどき **that made it a thousand francs** 合計が千フランになった

francs. And Her Highness refused to work. But she was always telling me that things were too tight, that she couldn't get by on what I was giving her. And I'd say to her, 'Why not work half-days? You'd be helping me out on all the little extras. I bought you a new outfit just this month, I give you twenty francs a day, I pay your rent, and what do you do? . . . You have coffee in the afternoons with your friends. You even provide the coffee and sugar. And me, I provide the money. I've been good to you, and this is how you repay me.' But she wouldn't work; she just kept on telling me she couldn't make ends meet—and that's what made me realize she was cheating on me."

Then he told me that he'd found a lottery ticket in her purse and she hadn't been able to explain how she paid for it. A short time later he'd found a ticket from the shop in Mont-de-Piété in her room which proved that she'd pawned two bracelets. Until then he hadn't even known the bracelets existed. "It was clear that she was cheating on me. So I left her. But first I smacked her around. And then I told her exactly what I thought of her. I told her that all she was interested in was getting into the sack. You see, Monsieur Meursault, it's like I told her: 'You don't realize that everybody's jealous of how good you have it with me. Someday you'll know just how good it was.' "

He'd beaten her till she bled. He'd never beaten her before. "I'd smack her around a little, but nice-like, you might say. She'd scream a little. I'd close the shutters

1 **Her Highness**（皮肉をこめて）女王　2 **things were too tight** 生活がとても苦しい　3 **get by** 生活していく　4 **You'd be helping me out on all the little extras** 少しは稼いでおれを助けてもいいだろう　5 **outfit** 服を一式、ひとそろい　7 **what do you do?** おまえはなにをしている？　10 **this is how you repay me** これがおれに対する礼だ　11 **make ends meet** やりくりする

14 **lottery ticket** 宝くじ　16 **a ticket** 質札　17 **Mont-de-Piété** 公営の質屋　**which**（先行詞は a ticket）18 **pawned** 質に入れた　20 **smacked her around** 引っぱたく　22 **getting into the sack** セックスをする　23 **it's like I told her** こんなふうに女にいってやった　25 **how good you have it with me** おれといることでどんなに幸せか

27 **beaten** 激しく殴った　**bled** 血が流れた　28 **I'd smack her around a little**（I'd は I would で、この would は習慣を表す）女を軽く引っぱたくことがよくあった　**nice-like** 軽く　**you might say** いってみれば　29 **I'd close the shutters and it always ended the same way.** おれが雨戸を閉めて、いつもならそれで終わりだ

and it always ended the same way. But this time it's for real. And if you ask me, she still hasn't gotten what she has coming."

Then he explained that that was what he needed advice about. He stopped to adjust the lamp's wick, which was smoking. I just listened. I'd drunk close to a liter of wine and my temples were burning. I was smoking Raymond's cigarettes because I'd run out. The last streetcars were going by, taking the now distant sounds of the neighborhood with them. Raymond went on. What bothered him was that he "still had sexual feelings for her." But he wanted to punish her. First he'd thought of taking her to a hotel and calling the vice squad to cause a scandal and have her listed as a common prostitute. After that he'd looked up some of his underworld friends. But they didn't come up with anything. As Raymond pointed out to me, a lot of good it does being in the underworld. He'd said the same thing to them, and then they'd suggested "marking" her. But that wasn't what he wanted. He was going to think about it. But first he wanted to ask me something. Before he did, though, he wanted to know what I thought of the whole thing. I said I didn't think anything but that it was interesting. He asked if I thought she was cheating on him, and it seemed to me she was; if I thought she should be punished and what I would do in his place, and I said you can't ever be sure, but I understood his wanting to punish her. I drank a little more wine. He lit a cigarette and let me in on what he was thinking about doing. He

1 **it's for real** 真剣だ　2 **And if you ask me** いわせてもらうが **she still hasn't gotten what she has coming** あの女はまだ十分な報いを受けていない
5 **stopped** 話をやめた　**adjust the lamp's wick** ランプの芯を調整した　7 **my temples were burning** こめかみが焼けるように熱かった　8 **because I'd run out** 自分のタバコがなくなったので　9 **taking the now distant sounds of the neighborhood with them** もう遠くなった近隣の音もいっしょに運んでいった　13 **the vice squad** 警察の風俗犯罪取締官　14 **common prostitute** 街娼、街角の売春婦　15 **looked up** 訪ねていった　**underworld friends** 裏社会の仲間　16 **didn't come up with anything** 何も思いつかなかった　17 **a lot of good it does being in the underworld**（it は being in the underworld）裏社会にいるといいことがたくさんある（皮肉でいっている）19 **marking** 刺青　23 **I didn't think anything but that it was interesting** じつにおもしろいと思う　25 **if I thought she should be punished and what I would do in his place** 彼女は罰せられるべきだと思うか、そしておれの立場だったらどうするか（と彼はたずねた）27 **you can't ever be sure**（you は一般人称）だれにもわからない　**but I understood his wanting to punish her** 彼女を罰したい気持ちはわかる　29 **let me in on what...** what 以下のことを私に打ち明けた

wanted to write her a letter, "one with a punch and also some things in it to make her sorry for what she's done." Then, when she came running back, he'd go to bed with her and "right at the last minute" he'd spit in her face and throw her out. Yes, that would punish her, I thought. But Raymond told me he didn't think he could write the kind of letter it would take and that he'd thought of asking me to write it for him. Since I didn't say anything, he asked if I'd mind doing it right then and I said no.

He downed a glass of wine and then stood up. He pushed aside the plates and the little bit of cold sausage we'd left. He carefully wiped the oilcloth covering the table. Then from a drawer in his night table he took out a sheet of paper, a yellow envelope, a small red pen box, and a square bottle with purple ink in it. When he told me the woman's name I realized she was Moorish. I wrote the letter. I did it just as it came to me, but I tried my best to please Raymond because I didn't have any reason not to please him. Then I read it out loud. He listened, smoking and nodding his head; then he asked me to read it again. He was very pleased. He said, "I could tell you knew about these things." I didn't notice at first, but he had stopped calling me "monsieur." It was only when he announced "Now you're a pal, Meursault" and said it again that it struck me. He repeated his remark and I said, "Yes." I didn't mind being his pal, and he seemed set on it. He sealed the letter and we finished off the wine. Then we sat and smoked for a while without saying anything. Outside, everything was quiet; we

1 **one with a punch**（one は letter）一撃を与えるような手紙 2 **some things in it to make her sorry** 彼女をほろっとさせるようなところもある 4 **right at the last minute**（right は強調）最後の最後に **spit** つばを吐く 5 **throw her out** 追い出す 6 **the kind of letter it would take** 効果のあるような手紙 8 **Since**（理由、原因を表す接続詞） 9 **he asked if I'd mind doing** やるのはいやかとたずねた **right then** すぐに **no**（no, I'd not mind doing）いやではない

10 **downed** 飲みほした 11 **plates** 皿 12 **oilcloth** テーブルクロス 16 **Moorish** ムーア人（アフリカ北西部に住むイスラム教徒） 22 **tell** わかる **knew about these things** こういうことをよく知っている 25 **said it again that it struck me** もう１度そういって、私を驚かせた **remark** 言葉 27 **set on it** 真剣にそう思っている **sealed the letter** 手紙に封をした

heard the sound of a car passing. I said, "It's late." Raymond thought so too. He remarked how quickly the time passed, and in a way it was true. I felt sleepy, but it was hard for me to get up. I must have looked tired, because Raymond told me not to let things get to me. At first I didn't understand. Then he explained that he'd heard about Maman's death but that it was one of those things that was bound to happen sooner or later. I thought so too.

I got up. Raymond gave me a very firm handshake and said that men always understand each other. I left his room, closing the door behind me, and paused for a minute in the dark, on the landing. The house was quiet, and a breath of dark, dank air wafted up from deep in the stairwell. All I could hear was the blood pounding in my ears. I stood there, motionless. And in old Salamano's room, the dog whimpered softly.

5 **let things get to me** 今の状況にくじける　8 **was bound to happen** 必ず起こる　**sooner or later** 遅かれ速かれ
13 **on the landing** 踊り場で　14 **dank air** 湿った風　**wafted up** ゆっくり吹き上がってきた　15 **stairwell** 階段の吹き抜け　**blood pounding** 脈が激しく打っている　17 **whimpered** くんくん鳴いていた

4

I worked hard all week. Raymond stopped by and told me he'd sent the letter. I went to the movies twice with Emmanuel, who doesn't always understand what's going on on the screen. So you have to explain things to him. Yesterday was Saturday, and Marie came over as we'd planned. I wanted her so bad when I saw her in that pretty red-and-white striped dress and leather sandals. You could make out the shape of her firm breasts, and her tan made her face look like a flower. We caught a bus and went a few kilometers outside Algiers, to a beach with rocks at either end, bordered by shore grass on the land side. The four o'clock sun wasn't too hot, but the water was warm, with slow, gently lapping waves. Marie taught me a game. As you swam, you had to skim off the foam from the crest of the waves with your mouth, hold it there, then roll over on your back and spout it out toward the sky. This made a delicate froth which disappeared into the air or fell back in a warm spray over my face. But after a while my mouth was stinging with the salty bitterness. Then Marie swam over to me and pressed herself against me in the water. She put her lips on mine. Her tongue cooled my lips and we tumbled in the waves for a moment.

When we'd gotten dressed again on the beach, Marie looked at me with her eyes sparkling. I kissed her. We didn't say anything more from that point on. I held her to me and we hurried to catch a bus, get back, go to my

3 **all week** その週はずっと　8 **wanted her so bad** 彼女を抱きたくてしょうがなかった　10 **make out** 見て取る　**firm breasts** かたい乳房　11 **tan** 日焼け　13 **shore grass** 浜辺の草　15 **lapping** ひたひた寄せる　17 **skim off the foam** 泡をすくい取る　**crest of the waves** 波頭　18 **hold it there** 口の中にためておく　19 **spout it out** 吐き出す　20 **froth** 泡　**fell back** 落ちてくる　21 **warm spray** 温かいしぶき　22 **stinging** ひりひりする　**salty bitterness** しょっぱい苦さ　23 **pressed herself against me** 私に体を押しつけてきた　25 **we tumbled** くるくる回った　27 **sparkling** 輝かせて　28 **from that point on** そのとき以降　**held her to me** 抱きしめていた

place, and throw ourselves onto my bed. I'd left my window open, and the summer night air flowing over our brown bodies felt good.

That morning Marie stayed and I told her that we would have lunch together. I went downstairs to buy some meat. On my way back upstairs I heard a woman's voice in Raymond's room. A little later old Salamano growled at his dog; we heard the sound of footsteps and claws on the wooden stairs and then "Lousy, stinking bastard" and they went down into the street. I told Marie all about the old man and she laughed. She was wearing a pair of my pajamas with the sleeves rolled up. When she laughed I wanted her again. A minute later she asked me if I loved her. I told her it didn't mean anything but that I didn't think so. She looked sad. But as we were fixing lunch, and for no apparent reason, she laughed in such a way that I kissed her. It was then that we heard what sounded like a fight break out in Raymond's room.

First we heard a woman's shrill voice and then Raymond saying, "You used me, you used me. I'll teach you to use me." There were some thuds and the woman screamed, but in such a terrifying way that the landing immediately filled with people. Marie and I went to see, too. The woman was still shrieking and Raymond was still hitting her. Marie said it was terrible and I didn't say anything. She asked me to go find a policeman, but I told her I didn't like cops. One showed up anyway with the tenant from the third floor, who's a plumber. The cop knocked on the door and we couldn't hear anything

2 **the summer night air flowing over our brown bodies** 私たちの日焼けした体をなでていく夏の夜風
8 **growled** 怒鳴った　9 **claws** 爪　12 **rolled up** まくりあげた
14 **it didn't mean anything but** 愛しているかどうかなんてどうでもいいことだが　15 **that I didn't think so** 自分はそう思っていない、君を愛していない　16 **fixing lunch** 昼食を作る　**for no apparent reason** これといった理由もないのに　**in such a way that**（way の前に lovely とか charming を補って考えるとわかりやすい）　17 **It was then that**（It was...that の強調構文）
19 **shrill** かん高い　20 **used** 利用した、食い物にした
21 **thuds** 鈍い音（殴る音）　22 **in such a terrifying way that** とてもすさまじかったので　24 **shrieking** 泣き叫んでいる
27 **cops** 警官　**One** =A cop　**showed up** 現れた、やってきた
28 **tenant** 借家人　**plumber** 鉛管工

anymore. He knocked harder and after a minute the woman started crying and Raymond opened the door. He had a cigarette in his mouth and an innocent look on his face. The girl rushed to the door and told the policeman that Raymond had hit her. "What's your name?" the cop said. Raymond told him. "Take that cigarette out of your mouth when you're talking to me," the cop said. Raymond hesitated, looked at me, and took a drag on his cigarette. Right then the cop slapped him—a thick, heavy smack right across the face. The cigarette went flying across the landing. The look on Raymond's face changed, but he didn't say anything for a minute, and then he asked, in a meek voice, if he could pick up his cigarette. The cop said to go ahead and added, "Next time you'll know better than to clown around with a policeman." Meanwhile the girl was crying and she repeated, "He beat me up! He's a pimp!" "Officer," Raymond asked, "is that legal, calling a man a pimp like that?" But the cop ordered him to shut his trap. Then Raymond turned to the girl and said, "You just wait, sweetheart—we're not through yet." The cop told him to knock it off and said that the girl was to go and he was to stay in his room and wait to be summoned to the police station. He also said that Raymond ought to be ashamed to be so drunk that he'd have the shakes like that. Then Raymond explained, "I'm not drunk, officer. It's just that I'm here, and you're there, and I'm shaking, I can't help it." He shut his door and everybody went away. Marie and I finished fixing lunch. But she wasn't hungry; I ate

8 **took a drag on his cigarette** タバコをひと吸いした 9 **Right then** ちょうどそのとき **slapped** 平手打ちした 10 **thick** 強烈な 13 **meek** おとなしい 14 **go ahead** 好きにしろ、吸いたければ吸え 15 **know better than** 慎重にする、分別をわきまえる **clown around** ふざける 16 **Meanwhile** 一方、その間 17 **Officer** お巡りさん 18 **legal** 合法 **calling a man a pimp** 人をポン引き呼ばわりする 19 **trap** 口 21 **we're not through yet** まだおれたちは終わってない **knock it off** 黙れ 23 **summoned** 呼び出される **police station** 警察署 25 **shakes** ふるえていること、よろよろしていること 26 **It's just that** ただ that 以下のような状況なのだ 27 **I can't help it** それは自分にはどうしようもない

almost everything. She left at one o'clock and I slept awhile.

Around three o'clock there was a knock on my door and Raymond came in. I didn't get up. He sat down on the edge of my bed. He didn't say anything for a minute and I asked him how it had all gone. He told me that he'd done what he wanted to do but that she'd slapped him and so he'd beaten her up. I'd seen the rest. I told him it seemed to me that she'd gotten her punishment now and he ought to be happy. He thought so too, and he pointed out that the cop could do anything he wanted, it wouldn't change the fact that she'd gotten her beating. He added that he knew all about cops and how to handle them. Then he asked me if I'd expected him to hit the cop back. I said I wasn't expecting anything, and besides I didn't like cops. Raymond seemed pretty happy. He asked me if I wanted to go for a walk with him. I got up and started combing my hair. He told me that I'd have to act as a witness for him. It didn't matter to me, but I didn't know what I was supposed to say. According to Raymond, all I had to do was to state that the girl had cheated on him. I agreed to act as a witness for him.

We went out and Raymond bought me a brandy. Then he wanted to shoot a game of pool, and I just barely lost. Afterwards he wanted to go to a whorehouse, but I said no, because I don't like that. So we took our time getting back, him telling me how glad he was that he'd been able to give the woman what she deserved. I found

6 **asked him how it had all gone** あの件はどうなったかたずねた　7 **what he wanted to do** 自分のやりたかったこと　**that**（前にHe toldを補う）　8 **the rest** そのあとのこと　10 **ought to be happy** 満足するべきだ　12 **she'd gotten her beating** 十分殴られた　19 **witness for him** 彼の証人になる　20 **was supposed to say** 何をいうべきか　21 **state** 述べる
25 **shoot a game of pool** プール（玉突きの一種）をやった　**just barely** おしいところで　26 **lost** 負けた　**whorehouse** 売春宿　28 **him telling me** 彼は私にいった　29 **give the woman what she deserved** あの女に思い知らせてやった

him very friendly with me and I thought it was a nice moment.

From a distance I noticed old Salamano standing on the doorstep. He looked flustered. When we got closer, I saw that he didn't have his dog. He was looking all over the place, turning around, peering into the darkness of the entryway, muttering incoherently, and then he started searching the street again with his little red eyes. When Raymond asked him what was wrong, he didn't answer right away. I barely heard him mumble "Stinking bastard," and he went on fidgeting around. I asked him where his dog was. He snapped at me and said he was gone. And then all of a sudden the words came pouring out: "I took him to the Parade Ground, like always. There were lots of people around the booths at the fair. I stopped to watch 'The King of the Escape Artists.' And when I was ready to go, he wasn't there. Sure, I've been meaning to get him a smaller collar for a long time. But I never thought the bastard would take off like that."

Then Raymond pointed out to him that the dog might have gotten lost and that he would come back. He gave examples of dogs that had walked dozens of kilometers to get back to their masters. Nevertheless, the old man looked even more flustered. "But they'll take him away from me, don't you see? If only somebody would take him in. But that's impossible—everybody's disgusted by his scabs. The police'll get him for sure." So I told him he should go to the pound and they'd give the dog back to him after he paid a fee. He asked me if it was a

4 **doorstep** 玄関前の階段 **flustered** 動揺している 5 **all over the place** いたるところ 7 **entryway** 通路 **muttering incoherently** 意味のわからないことをつぶやいている 9 **what was wrong** どうしたんだ 10 **Stinking bastard** いまいましいやつ（飼っているスパニエル犬のこと） 11 **fidgeting** 不安そうにしている 12 **snapped at me** 噛みついた、怒鳴った 14 **the Parade Ground** 練兵場 15 **booths** 売店、屋台 **fair** 縁日、定期市 16 **The King of the Escape Artists**「脱出王」 18 **meaning to get him a smaller collar** あいつにもっと小さい首輪をつけてやろうと思っていた 19 **the bastard** 犬のこと **take off** 逃げる

21 **gotten lost** 迷った 22 **dozens of kilometers** 何十キロも 25 **If only** ～ならいいのに **take him in** 引き取ってくれる 27 **scabs** かさぶた **for sure** まちがいなく 28 **pound** 動物収容所 29 **fee** 手数料

big fee. I didn't know. Then he got mad: "Pay money for that bastard—ha! He can damn well die!" And he started cursing the dog. Raymond laughed and went inside. I followed him and we parted upstairs on the landing. A minute later I heard the old man's footsteps and he knocked on my door. When I opened it, he stood in the doorway for a minute and said, "Excuse me, excuse me." I asked him to come in, but he refused. He was looking down at the tips of his shoes and his scabby hands were trembling. Without looking up at me he asked, "They're not going to take him away from me, are they, Monsieur Meursault? They'll give him back to me. Otherwise, what's going to happen to me?" I told him that the pound kept dogs for three days so that their owners could come and claim them and that after that they did with them as they saw fit. He looked at me in silence. Then he said, "Good night." He shut his door and I heard him pacing back and forth. His bed creaked. And from the peculiar little noise coming through the partition, I realized he was crying. For some reason I thought of Maman. But I had to get up early the next morning. I wasn't hungry, and I went to bed without any dinner.

1 **got mad** 怒った　2 **He can damn well die!** あんなやつは死んじまえばいい！　9 **tips of his shoes** 靴の先　**scabby** かさぶたのある、傷だらけの　13 **Otherwise** そうでなかったら　**what's going to happen to me?** いったい、自分はどうなってしまうか　15 **after that** そのあとは　16 **they did with them as they saw fit**（they は動物収容所の人）彼らが自分たちのいいと思うようにする　18 **pacing back and forth** 歩きまわる　19 **peculiar** 奇妙な　**through the partition** 仕切りのむこうから

5

Raymond called me at the office. He told me that a friend of his (he'd spoken to him about me) had invited me to spend the day Sunday at his little beach house, near Algiers. I said I'd really like to, but I'd promised to spend the day with a girlfriend. Raymond immediately told me that she was invited too. His friend's wife would be very glad not to be alone with a bunch of men.

I wanted to hang up right away because I know the boss doesn't like people calling us from town. But Raymond asked me to hang on and told me he could have passed on the invitation that evening, but he had something else to tell me. He'd been followed all day by a group of Arabs, one of whom was the brother of his former mistress. "If you see him hanging around the building when you get home this evening, let me know." I said I would.

A little later my boss sent for me, and for a second I was annoyed, because I thought he was going to tell me to do less talking on the phone and more work. But that wasn't it at all. He told me he wanted to talk to me about a plan of his that was still pretty vague. He just wanted to have my opinion on the matter. He was planning to open an office in Paris which would handle his business directly with the big companies, on the spot, and he wanted to know how I felt about going there. I'd be able to live in Paris and to travel around for part of the year as well. "You're young, and it seems to me it's the

9 **a bunch of men** 大勢の男
12 **he could have passed on the invitation that evening** この招待は夜になって伝えることもできた 14 **been followed** 尾行された 18 **would** would let you know
19 **sent for me** 私を呼びに人をよこした 21 **that wasn't it at all** そんなことではまったくなかった 23 **vague** ぼんやりした、まとまっていない 24 **on the matter** その件について 26 **on the spot** 現地で 28 **for part of the year** 一年の一定の期間
29 **as well** そのうえ

kind of life that would appeal to you." I said yes but that really it was all the same to me. Then he asked me if I wasn't interested in a change of life. I said that people never change their lives, that in any case one life was as good as another and that I wasn't dissatisfied with mine here at all. He looked upset and told me that I never gave him a straight answer, that I had no ambition, and that that was disastrous in business. So I went back to work. I would rather not have upset him, but I couldn't see any reason to change my life. Looking back on it, I wasn't unhappy. When I was a student, I had lots of ambitions like that. But when I had to give up my studies I learned very quickly that none of it really mattered.

That evening Marie came by to see me and asked me if I wanted to marry her. I said it didn't make any difference to me and that we could if she wanted to. Then she wanted to know if I loved her. I answered the same way I had the last time, that it didn't mean anything but that I probably didn't love her. "So why marry me, then?" she said. I explained to her that it didn't really matter and that if she wanted to, we could get married. Besides, she was the one who was doing the asking and all I was saying was yes. Then she pointed out that marriage was a serious thing. I said, "No." She stopped talking for a minute and looked at me without saying anything. Then she spoke. She just wanted to know if I would have accepted the same proposal from another woman, with whom I was involved in the same way. I said, "Sure." Then she said she wondered if she loved me, and there

3 **people never change their lives** 人というものは決して生活を変えないものだ　4 **in any case** どんな場合であれ、ともかく **one life was as good as another** どんな生活も似たようなもの 5 **mine here** ここでの自分の生活　6 **looked upset** 驚いたようだった　**told me** 私に話した内容は、そのあとの３つの that 以下（① that I never... ② that I had... ③ that that was...）　8 **disastrous** 致命的にまずい　13 **none of it really mattered** そんなことはまったくどうでもいい

20 **it didn't really matter** じつは、そんなことは（なぜ結婚するかということは）どうでもいい　21 **Besides** そのうえ　22 **she was the one who was doing the asking** 彼女がその質問をした当人だった　**all I was saying was yes** 私は（それに対して）yes といっているだけだ　27 **with whom I was involved in the same way** 私が同じような状況になった相手に対して　29 **wondered** ～かどうか不安だ、わからない

was no way I could know about that. After another moment's silence, she mumbled that I was peculiar, that that was probably why she loved me but that one day I might hate her for the same reason. I didn't say anything, because I didn't have anything to add, so she took my arm with a smile and said she wanted to marry me. I said we could do it whenever she wanted. Then I told her about my boss's proposition and she said she'd love to see Paris. I told her that I'd lived there once and she asked me what it was like. I said, "It's dirty. Lots of pigeons and dark courtyards. Everybody's pale."

Then we went for a walk through the main streets to the other end of town. The women were beautiful and I asked Marie if she'd noticed. She said yes and that she understood what I meant. For a while neither of us said anything. But I wanted her to stay with me, and I told her we could have dinner together at Céleste's. She would have liked to but she had something to do. We were near my place and I said goodbye to her. She looked at me. "Don't you want to know what I have to do?" I did, but I hadn't thought to ask, and she seemed to be scolding me. Then, seeing me so confused, she laughed again and she moved toward me with her whole body to offer me her lips.

I had dinner at Céleste's. I'd already started eating when a strange little woman came in and asked me if she could sit at my table. Of course she could. Her gestures were jerky and she had bright eyes in a little face like an apple. She took off her jacket, sat down, and

2 **peculiar** 変わっている　11 **pale** 色白
22 **seeing me so confused** 私がとてもこまっているのがわかると
28 **jerky** ぎくしゃくしている

studied the menu feverishly. She called Céleste over and ordered her whole meal all at once, in a voice that was clear and very fast at the same time. While she was waiting for her first course, she opened her bag, took out a slip of paper and a pencil, added up the bill in advance, then took the exact amount, plus tip, out of a vest pocket and set it down on the table in front of her. At that point the waiter brought her first course and she gulped it down. While waiting for the next course, she again took out of her bag a blue pencil and a magazine that listed the radio programs for the week. One by one, and with great care, she checked off almost every program. Since the magazine was about a dozen pages long, she meticulously continued this task throughout the meal. I had already finished and she was still checking away with the same zeal. Then she stood up, put her jacket back on with the same robotlike movements, and left. I didn't have anything to do, so I left too and followed her for a while. She had positioned herself right next to the curb and was making her way with incredible speed and assurance, never once swerving or looking around. I eventually lost sight of her and turned back. I thought about how peculiar she was but forgot about her a few minutes later.

I found old Salamano waiting outside my door. I asked him in and he told me that his dog was lost, because it wasn't at the pound. The people who worked there had told him that maybe it had been run over. He asked if he could find out at the police station. They told

1 **studied the menu** メニューを読んだ **feverishly** 熱心に 2 **all at once** 全部いっしょに 5 **a slip of paper** 1枚の紙 **added up the bill** 料金を足して **in advance** 前もって 6 **exact amount** きっちりの金額 8 **At that point** そのとき 9 **gulped it down** 噛まずに飲みこんだ 12 **with great care** とてもていねいに 13 **Since**（理由、原因を表す接続詞） 14 **meticulously** 細かく 16 **zeal** 熱意 17 **robotlike** ロボットのような 19 **positioned herself** ～にいた 20 **next to the curb** 歩道の縁石の脇 21 **assurance** 確実さ、正確さ **swerving** それる、はずれる

28 **had been run over** 車にひかれた

him that they didn't keep track of things like that because they happened every day. I told old Salamano that he could get another dog, but he was right to point out to me that he was used to this one.

I was sitting cross-legged on my bed and Salamano had sat down on a chair in front of the table. He was facing me and he had both hands on his knees. He had kept his old felt hat on. He was mumbling bits and pieces of sentences through his yellowing moustache. He was getting on my nerves a little, but I didn't have anything to do and I didn't feel sleepy. Just for something to say, I asked him about his dog. He told me he'd gotten it after his wife died. He had married fairly late. When he was young he'd wanted to go into the theater: in the army he used to act in military vaudevilles. But he had ended up working on the railroads, and he didn't regret it, because now he had a small pension. He hadn't been happy with his wife, but he'd pretty much gotten used to her. When she died he had been very lonely. So he asked a shop buddy for a dog and he'd gotten this one very young. He'd had to feed it from a bottle. But since a dog doesn't live as long as a man, they'd ended up being old together. "He was bad-tempered," Salamano said. "We'd have a run-in every now and then. But he was a good dog just the same." I said he was well bred and Salamano looked pleased. "And," he added, "you didn't know him before he got sick. His coat was the best thing about him." Every night and every morning after the dog had gotten that skin disease, Salamano

1 **didn't keep track of things like that** そのようなことは記録に残していない
8 **mumbling** もごもご話す　10 **getting on my nerves** 私の気に触るようになってきた　13 **fairly** かなり　14 **go into the theater** 舞台に立つ　15 **vaudevilles** ヴォードヴィル（歌や踊りやお笑いなどのショー）　16 **working on the railroads** 鉄道関係の仕事　17 **pension** 恩給、年金　18 **he'd pretty much gotten used to her** 妻に（結婚生活に）はかなり慣れていた　20 **shop buddy** 仕事仲間　**this one** いま飼っている犬　21 **feed it from a bottle** 哺乳瓶でミルクをやった　22 **since**（理由、原因を表す接続詞）　23 **bad-tempered** 怒りっぽい　24 **a run-in** けんか　25 **just the same** それにもかかわらず、それでも　**was well bred** 育ちがいい　27 **you didn't know him before he got sick** あんたは、病気になるまえのあいつを知らない　**His coat** 毛並み

rubbed him with ointment. But according to him, the dog's real sickness was old age, and there's no cure for old age.

At that point I yawned, and the old man said he'd be going. I told him that he could stay and that I was sorry about what had happened to his dog. He thanked me. He told me that Maman was very fond of his dog. He called her "your poor mother." He said he supposed I must be very sad since Maman died, and I didn't say anything. Then he said, very quickly and with an embarrassed look, that he realized that some people in the neighborhood thought badly of me for having sent Maman to the home, but he knew me and he knew I loved her very much. I still don't know why, but I said that until then I hadn't realized that people thought badly of me for doing it, but that the home had seemed like the natural thing since I didn't have enough money to have Maman cared for. "Anyway," I added, "it had been a long time since she'd had anything to say to me, and she was bored all by herself." "Yes," he said, "and at least in a home you can make a few friends." Then he said good night. He wanted to sleep. His life had changed now and he wasn't too sure what he was going to do. For the first time since I'd known him, and with a furtive gesture, he offered me his hand, and I felt the scales on his skin. He gave a little smile, and before he left he said, "I hope the dogs don't bark tonight. I always think it's mine."

1 **ointment** 軟膏　2 **no cure** 治療法なし
10 **with an embarrassed look** こまったような顔で
12 **thought badly of me** あんたのことを悪く思っている
17 **enough money to have Maman cared for** 母親の面倒をみてもらうのに十分な金　20 **by herself** ひとりきりでいること
24 **with a furtive gesture** おずおずとした仕草で　25 **scales** 荒れた肌

6

I had a hard time waking up on Sunday, and Marie had to call me and shake me. We didn't eat anything, because we wanted to get to the beach early. I felt completely drained and I had a slight headache. My cigarette tasted bitter. Marie made fun of me because, she said, I had on a "funeral face." She had put on a white linen dress and let her hair down. I told her she was beautiful and she laughed with delight.

On our way downstairs we knocked on Raymond's door. He told us he'd be right down. Once out in the street, because I was so tired and also because we hadn't opened the blinds, the day, already bright with sun, hit me like a slap in the face. Marie was jumping with joy and kept on saying what a beautiful day it was. I felt a little better and I noticed that I was hungry. I told Marie, who pointed to her oilcloth bag where she'd put our bathing suits and a towel. I just had to wait and then we heard Raymond shutting his door. He had on blue trousers and a white short-sleeved shirt. But he'd put on a straw hat, which made Marie laugh, and his forearms were all white under the black hairs. I found it a little repulsive. He was whistling as he came down the stairs and he seemed very cheerful. He said "Good morning, old man" to me and called Marie "mademoiselle."

The day before, we'd gone to the police station and I'd testified that the girl had cheated on Raymond. He'd gotten off with a warning. They didn't check out my

3 **had a hard time waking up** 起きるのがつらかった
6 **drained** ぐったり疲れている 7 **made fun** からかった
12 **be right down** すぐに下りていく 18 **oilcloth** 油布、オイルクロス 22 **forearms were all white under the black hairs** 前腕は白くて、黒い毛におおわれている 24 **repulsive** 気持ち悪い **was whistling** 口笛を吹いていた
28 **testified** 証言した 29 **gotten off with a warning** 警告を受けて釈放された **check out** 調べる

statement. Outside the front door we talked about it with Raymond, and then we decided to take the bus. The beach wasn't very far, but we'd get there sooner that way. Raymond thought his friend would be glad to see us get there early. We were just about to leave when all of a sudden Raymond motioned to me to look across the street. I saw a group of Arabs leaning against the front of the tobacconist's shop. They were staring at us in silence, but in that way of theirs, as if we were nothing but stones or dead trees. Raymond told me that the second one from the left was his man, and he seemed worried. But, he added, it was all settled now. Marie didn't really understand and asked us what was wrong. I told her that they were Arabs who had it in for Raymond. She wanted to get going right away. Raymond drew himself up and laughed, saying we'd better step on it.

We headed toward the bus stop, which wasn't far, and Raymond said that the Arabs weren't following us. I turned around. They were still in the same place and they were looking with the same indifference at the spot where we'd just been standing. We caught the bus. Raymond, who seemed very relieved, kept on cracking jokes for Marie. I could tell he liked her, but she hardly said anything to him. Every once in a while she'd look at him and laugh.

We got off in the outskirts of Algiers. The beach wasn't far from the bus stop. But we had to cross a small plateau which overlooks the sea and then drops steeply down to the beach. It was covered with yellowish rocks

1 **statement** 証言 6 **motioned** 仕草で伝えた 7 **leaning against** もたれている 11 **his man** あの男、例の男 14 **had it in for** ～に恨みを持っている 15 **get going right away** すぐに出発する **drew himself up** 胸を張った 16 **step on it** 急ぐ 20 **indifference** 無関心 22 **relieved** ほっとした **cracking jokes** 冗談を飛ばす 23 **tell** わかる 24 **Every once in a while** たまに
28 **plateau** 台地

and the whitest asphodels set against the already hard blue of the sky. Marie was having fun scattering the petals, taking big swipes at them with her oilcloth bag. We walked between rows of small houses behind green or white fences, some with their verandas hidden behind the tamarisks, others standing naked among the rocks. Before we reached the edge of the plateau, we could already see the motionless sea and, farther out, a massive, drowsy-looking promontory in the clear water. The faint hum of a motor rose up to us in the still air. And way off, we saw a tiny trawler moving, almost imperceptibly, across the dazzling sea. Marie gathered some rock irises. From the slope leading down to the beach, we could see that there were already some people swimming.

Raymond's friend lived in a little wooden bungalow at the far end of the beach. The back of the house rested up against the rocks, and the pilings that held it up in front went straight down into the water. Raymond introduced us. His friend's name was Masson. He was a big guy, very tall and broad-shouldered, with a plump, sweet little wife with a Parisian accent. Right off he told us to make ourselves at home and said that his wife had just fried up some fish he'd caught that morning. I told him how nice I thought his house was. He told me that he spent Saturdays and Sundays and all his days off there. "With my wife, of course," he added. Just then his wife was laughing with Marie. For the first time maybe, I really thought I was going to get married.

1 **asphodels** アスフォデル（ユリ科の植物） **hard blue** 強烈なブルー 2 **Marie was having fun** マリーは楽しんでいた **scattering the petals** 花びらを散らすこと 3 **taking big swipes at them with her oilcloth bag** 油布のバッグでアスフォデルを乱暴になぐること 6 **tamarisks** ギョリュウ（10mほどに育つ） **others** other houses **naked** 低木などにおおわれないで 8 **massive** 堂々とした 9 **drowsy-looking promontory** 眠そうにみえる岬 10 **faint hum** かすかなうなり **rose up to us** 私たちのところに下から響いてきた **still** 静止している、動かない 11 **way off** むこうのほうに **trawler** トロール船 **imperceptibly** わからない程度に 12 **dazzling** まぶしい 13 **rock irises** イチハツ（アイリス、アヤメの一種で紫の花が咲く）

18 **pilings** 支柱、杭 **held it up** 支えていた 21 **plump** ぽっちゃりした 22 **sweet little wife** かわいい小柄な妻 **Parisian accent** パリのアクセント **Right off** すぐに 26 **all his days off** 彼の休みの日すべて

Masson wanted to go for a swim, but his wife and Raymond didn't want to come. The three of us went down to the beach and Marie jumped right in. Masson and I waited a little. He spoke slowly, and I noticed that he had a habit of finishing everything he said with "and I'd even say," when really it didn't add anything to the meaning of his sentence. Referring to Marie, he said, "She's stunning, and I'd even say charming." After that I didn't pay any more attention to this mannerism of his, because I was absorbed by the feeling that the sun was doing me a lot of good. The sand was starting to get hot underfoot. I held back the urge to get into the water a minute longer, but finally I said to Masson, "Shall we?" I dove in. He waded in slowly and started swimming only when he couldn't touch bottom anymore. He did the breast stroke, and not too well, either, so I left him and joined Marie. The water was cold and I was glad to be swimming. Together again, Marie and I swam out a ways, and we felt a closeness as we moved in unison and were happy.

Out in deeper water we floated on our backs and the sun on my upturned face was drying the last of the water trickling into my mouth. We saw Masson making his way back to the beach to stretch out in the sun. From far away he looked huge. Marie wanted us to swim together. I got behind her to hold her around the waist. She used her arms to move us forward and I did the kicking. The little splashing sound followed us through the morning air until I got tired. I left Marie and headed

6 **I'd even say** といってもいいだろう　8 **stunning** 素晴らしい、とても魅力的な　9 **this mannerism of his** 彼のこういった癖　10 **I was absorbed** うっとりしていた　12 **held back the urge** ～したい気持ちをおさえていた　13 **Shall we?** いきませんか？　14 **waded in** 歩いて海に入ってきた　15 **couldn't touch bottom anymore** 足が下につかなくなった　16 **breast stroke** 平泳ぎ　18 **swam out a ways** 沖まで泳いでいった　19 **closeness** 親密さ　**in unison** いっしょに
22 **upturned** 上を向いた　23 **trickling into** 流れこんでくる　24 **stretch out** 体を伸ばす　26 **hold her around the waist** 彼女の腰を抱く　28 **splashing** 水音

back, swimming smoothly and breathing easily. On the beach I stretched out on my stomach alongside Masson and put my face on the sand. I said it was nice and he agreed. Soon afterwards Marie came back. I rolled over to watch her coming. She was glistening all over with salty water and holding her hair back. She lay down right next to me and the combined warmth from her body and from the sun made me doze off.

Marie shook me and told me that Masson had gone back up to the house, that it was time for lunch. I got up right away because I was hungry, but Marie told me I hadn't kissed her since that morning. It was true, and yet I had wanted to. "Come into the water," she said. We ran and threw ourselves into the first little waves. We swam a few strokes and she reached out and held on to me. I felt her legs wrapped around mine and I wanted her.

When we got back, Masson was already calling us. I said I was starving and then out of the blue he announced to his wife that he liked me. The bread was good; I devoured my share of the fish. After that there was some meat and fried potatoes. We all ate without talking. Masson drank a lot of wine and kept filling my glass. By the time the coffee came, my head felt heavy and I smoked a lot. Masson, Raymond, and I talked about spending August together at the beach, sharing expenses. Suddenly Marie said, "Do you know what time it is? It's only eleven-thirty!" We were all surprised, but Masson said that we'd eaten very early and that it was

4 **rolled over** 転がった 7 **the combined warmth from her body and from the sun** 彼女の体の温かさと太陽の温かさがいっしょになったもの 8 **doze off** うつらうつらする
15 **reached out** 手をのばした **held on to me** 私にしっかりつかまった
19 **out of the blue** 突然 21 **devoured** がつがつ食べた

only natural because lunchtime was whenever you were hungry. For some reason that made Marie laugh. I think she'd had a little too much to drink. Then Masson asked me if I wanted to go for a walk on the beach with him. "My wife always takes a nap after lunch. Me, I don't like naps. I need to walk. I tell her all the time it's better for her health. But it's her business." Marie said she'd stay and help Madame Masson with the dishes. The little Parisienne said that first they'd have to get rid of the men. The three of us went down to the beach.

The sun was shining almost directly overhead onto the sand, and the glare on the water was unbearable. There was no one left on the beach. From inside the bungalows bordering the plateau and jutting out over the water, we could hear the rattling of plates and silverware. It was hard to breathe in the rocky heat rising from the ground. At first Raymond and Masson discussed people and things I didn't know about. I gathered they'd known each other for a long time and had even lived together at one point. We headed down to the sea and walked along the water's edge. Now and then a little wave would come up higher than the others and wet our canvas shoes. I wasn't thinking about anything, because I was half asleep from the sun beating down on my bare head.

At that point Raymond said something to Masson which I didn't quite catch. But at the same time I noticed, at the far end of the beach and a long way from us, two Arabs in blue overalls coming in our direction.

2 **For some reason** なぜか　7 **it's her business** 彼女が決めればいいこと　8 **help Madame Masson with the dishes** マダム・マソンが食器を片づける手伝いをする　9 **get rid of the men** 男たちをやっかいばらいする

14 **plateau** 台地　**jutting out** 突き出ている　16 **silverware** 銀器、ナイフやフォークやスプーン　**the rocky heat**（日にあぶられた）岩の熱　18 **gathered** 推測した　20 **at one point** ある時期　22 **the others** the other little waves　23 **canvas shoes** ズック靴　24 **beating down** 照りつけている　25 **bare head** 帽子をかぶっていない頭

27 **catch** 聞き取る　29 **in blue overalls** 青いオーバーオールを着ている

I looked at Raymond and he said, "It's him." We kept walking. Masson asked how they'd managed to follow us all this way. I thought they must have seen us get on the bus with a beach bag, but I didn't say anything.

The Arabs were walking slowly, but they were already much closer. We didn't change our pace, but Raymond said, "If there's any trouble, Masson, you take the other one. I'll take care of my man. Meursault, if another one shows up, he's yours." I said, "Yes," and Masson put his hands in his pockets. The blazing sand looked red to me now. We moved steadily toward the Arabs. The distance between us was getting shorter and shorter. When we were just a few steps away from each other, the Arabs stopped. Masson and I slowed down. Raymond went right up to his man. I couldn't hear what he said to him, but the other guy made a move as though he were going to butt him. Then Raymond struck the first blow and called Masson right away. Masson went for the one that had been pointed out as his and hit him twice, as hard as he could. The Arab fell flat in the water, facedown, and lay there for several seconds with bubbles bursting on the surface around his head. Meanwhile Raymond had landed one too, and the other Arab's face was bleeding. Raymond turned to me and said, "Watch this. I'm gonna let him have it now." I shouted, "Look out, he's got a knife!" But Raymond's arm had already been cut open and his mouth slashed. Masson lunged forward. But the other Arab had gotten back up and gone around behind the one with the knife. We didn't dare move. They

2 **managed to follow** あとを追ってやってこられた
8 **take care of my man** あの男（自分をつけねらっている男）の相手をする 9 **he's yours** おまえが彼の相手をしてくれ 10 **blazing** 輝く 17 **butt** 頭突きをする 18 **right away** すぐに **went for** ～に向かっていった **the one that had been pointed out as his** 相手をするように指示された男 20 **fell flat** 倒れた 22 **the surface** 水面 23 **landed** 殴った 24 **Watch this** これをみろよ 25 **let him have it** こいつに思い知らせてやる 27 **slashed** 切りつけられていた **lunged** 飛びだした 28 **gotten back up** 立ち上がっていた 29 **didn't dare move** 動くことができなかった

started backing off slowly, without taking their eyes off us, keeping us at bay with the knife. When they thought they were far enough away, they took off running as fast as they could while we stood there motionless in the sun and Raymond clutched at his arm dripping with blood.

Masson immediately said there was a doctor who spent his Sundays up on the plateau. Raymond wanted to go see him right away. But every time he tried to talk the blood bubbled in his mouth. We steadied him and made our way back to the bungalow as quickly as we could. Once there, Raymond said that they were only flesh wounds and that he could make it to the doctor's. He left with Masson and I stayed to explain to the women what had happened. Madame Masson was crying and Marie was very pale. I didn't like having to explain to them, so I just shut up, smoked a cigarette, and looked at the sea.

Raymond came back with Masson around one-thirty. His arm was bandaged up and he had an adhesive plaster on the corner of his mouth. The doctor had told him that it was nothing, but Raymond looked pretty grim. Masson tried to make him laugh. But he still wouldn't say anything. When he said he was going down to the beach, I asked him where he was going. He said he wanted to get some air. Masson and I said we'd go with him. But that made him angry and he swore at us. Masson said not to argue with him. I followed him anyway.

We walked on the beach for a long time. By now the

2 **keeping us at bay** 私たちを寄せつけない 5 **clutched at** つかんでいた **dripping with blood** 血が流れている
9 **bubbled** 泡になって流れ出た **steadied**（両側から）支えてやった 12 **make it to the doctor's** 医者のところまでいく
19 **bandaged** 包帯を巻かれた **adhesive plaster** 絆創膏
21 **pretty grim** とても不機嫌な 26 **swore** ののしった 27 **followed him** 彼のあとをついていった 29 **the sun** 日光

sun was overpowering. It shattered into little pieces on the sand and water. I had the impression that Raymond knew where he was going, but I was probably wrong. At the far end of the beach we finally came to a little spring running down through the sand behind a large rock. There we found our two Arabs. They were lying down, in their greasy overalls. They seemed perfectly calm and almost content. Our coming changed nothing. The one who had attacked Raymond was looking at him without saying anything. The other one was blowing through a little reed over and over again, watching us out of the corner of his eye. He kept repeating the only three notes he could get out of his instrument.

The whole time there was nothing but the sun and the silence, with the low gurgling from the spring and the three notes. Then Raymond put his hand in his hip pocket, but the others didn't move, they just kept looking at each other. I noticed that the toes on the one playing the flute were tensed. But without taking his eyes off his adversary, Raymond asked me, "Should I let him have it?" I thought that if I said no he'd get himself all worked up and shoot for sure. All I said was, "He hasn't said anything yet. It'd be pretty lousy to shoot him like that." You could still hear the sound of the water and the flute deep within the silence and the heat. Then Raymond said, "So I'll call him something and when he answers back, I'll let him have it." I answered, "Right. But if he doesn't draw his knife, you can't shoot." Raymond started getting worked up. The other Arab went

1 **overpowering** すさまじい **It shattered into little pieces** 日光が砕け散っていた 4 **spring** 泉 7 **greasy overalls** 油まみれのオーバーオール 10 **blowing through a little reed** 小さい葦笛を吹いている 11 **out of the corner of his eye** 目の端で 12 **notes** 音 13 **his instrument** 彼の楽器（葦笛）
15 **gurgling** 水音 18 **the toes** 足の指 19 **tensed** 緊張している、こわばっている 20 **adversary** 敵 **Should I let him have it?** やつに思い知らせてやるか？ 21 **get himself all worked up** 彼を興奮させる 22 **shoot** ピストルを撃つ **for sure** まちがいなく 23 **lousy** 卑劣な 24 **You**（一般人称） 26 **he answers back** 言い返す 29 **started getting worked up** 興奮してきた

on playing, and both of them were watching every move Raymond made. "No," I said to Raymond, "take him on man to man and give me your gun. If the other one moves in, or if he draws his knife, I'll let him have it."

The sun glinted off Raymond's gun as he handed it to me. But we just stood there motionless, as if everything had closed in around us. We stared at each other without blinking, and everything came to a stop there between the sea, the sand, and the sun, and the double silence of the flute and the water. It was then that I realized that you could either shoot or not shoot. But all of a sudden, the Arabs, backing away, slipped behind the rock. So Raymond and I turned and headed back the way we'd come. He seemed better and talked about the bus back.

I went with him as far as the bungalow, and as he climbed the wooden steps, I just stood there at the bottom, my head ringing from the sun, unable to face the effort it would take to climb the wooden staircase and face the women again. But the heat was so intense that it was just as bad standing still in the blinding stream falling from the sky. To stay or to go, it amounted to the same thing. A minute later I turned back toward the beach and started walking.

There was the same dazzling red glare. The sea gasped for air with each shallow, stifled little wave that broke on the sand. I was walking slowly toward the rocks and I could feel my forehead swelling under the sun. All that heat was pressing down on me and making it hard for me to go on. And every time I felt a blast of

2 **take him on man to man** 一対一で立ち向かえ
6 **everything had closed in around us** すべてがわれわれのまわりに迫ってきた 8 **blinking** まばたき 9 **the double silence of the flute and the water** 葦笛の音も水音もきこえない状態
11 **you**（一般人称） 14 **the bus back** 帰りのバス
17 **my head ringing from the sun** 陽に照りつけられて頭ががんがんしていた **unable to face the effort** 〜する気力がない 20 **blinding stream** まぶしい流れ 21 **it amounted to the same thing** 結局は、どちらも同じ
25 **gasped for air** 息をしようとあえいだ **shallow, stifled little wave** 浅く、息苦しそうな小波 27 **swelling** ふくれる
29 **blast** 突風、爆風

its hot breath strike my face, I gritted my teeth, clenched my fists in my trouser pockets, and strained every nerve in order to overcome the sun and the thick drunkenness it was spilling over me. With every blade of light that flashed off the sand, from a bleached shell or a piece of broken glass, my jaws tightened. I walked for a long time.

From a distance I could see the small, dark mass of rock surrounded by a blinding halo of light and sea spray. I was thinking of the cool spring behind the rock. I wanted to hear the murmur of its water again, to escape the sun and the strain and the women's tears, and to find shade and rest again at last. But as I got closer, I saw that Raymond's man had come back.

He was alone. He was lying on his back, with his hands behind his head, his forehead in the shade of the rock, the rest of his body in the sun. His blue overalls seemed to be steaming in the heat. I was a little surprised. As far as I was concerned, the whole thing was over, and I'd gone there without even thinking about it.

As soon as he saw me, he sat up a little and put his hand in his pocket. Naturally, I gripped Raymond's gun inside my jacket. Then he lay back again, but without taking his hand out of his pocket. I was pretty far away from him, about ten meters or so. I could tell he was glancing at me now and then through half-closed eyes. But most of the time, he was just a form shimmering before my eyes in the fiery air. The sound of the waves was even lazier, more drawn out than at noon. It was the

1 **gritted my teeth** 歯を食いしばった **clenched my fists** 両手を握りしめた 2 **strained every nerve** 全力をつくした 3 **thick drunkenness**（太陽の光に）酔っ払った状態 4 **spilling** 降りそそいでいる **blade** 刃 5 **flashed** 反射した **bleached** 白くなった
9 **halo** 光輪 **sea spray** 波のしぶき 11 **murmur** せせらぎ
15 **on his back** あお向けに 18 **steaming** 湯気が上がっている
19 **the whole thing was over** すべては終わっていた
21 **sat up** 体を起こした 24 **pretty** かなり 25 **tell** わかる
27 **form** 形、輪郭 **shimmering** ゆらめいている 28 **in the fiery air** 炎のような空気の中で 29 **drawn out** 間延びしていた

same sun, the same light still shining on the same sand as before. For two hours the day had stood still; for two hours it had been anchored in a sea of molten lead. On the horizon, a tiny steamer went by, and I made out the black dot from the corner of my eye because I hadn't stopped watching the Arab.

It occurred to me that all I had to do was turn around and that would be the end of it. But the whole beach, throbbing in the sun, was pressing on my back. I took a few steps toward the spring. The Arab didn't move. Besides, he was still pretty far away. Maybe it was the shadows on his face, but it looked like he was laughing. I waited. The sun was starting to burn my cheeks, and I could feel drops of sweat gathering in my eyebrows. The sun was the same as it had been the day I'd buried Maman, and like then, my forehead especially was hurting me, all the veins in it throbbing under the skin. It was this burning, which I couldn't stand anymore, that made me move forward. I knew that it was stupid, that I wouldn't get the sun off me by stepping forward. But I took a step, one step, forward. And this time, without getting up, the Arab drew his knife and held it up to me in the sun. The light shot off the steel and it was like a long flashing blade cutting at my forehead. At the same instant the sweat in my eyebrows dripped down over my eyelids all at once and covered them with a warm, thick film. My eyes were blinded behind the curtain of tears and salt. All I could feel were the cymbals of sunlight crashing on my forehead and, indistinctly, the

2 **stood still** じっと動かなかった 3 **anchored** 錨でつなぎ止められていた **molten lead** 溶けた鉛 4 **steamer** 蒸気船 **made out the black dot** 黒い点（のような蒸気船）がみえた
8 **that would be the end of it** そうすれば、これは終わる 9 **throbbing** 脈打っている **pressing on my back** 背中を押していた 17 **veins** 血管 18 **stand** 我慢する 20 **get the sun off me** 照りつける陽射しから逃れる 23 **The light shot off the steel** 鋼（ナイフ）がぎらっと光った 26 **them** eyelids 27 **film** 膜 28 **cymbals** シンバル 29 **crashing** 音を立ててぶつかる **indistinctly** ぼんやりと

dazzling spear flying up from the knife in front of me. The scorching blade slashed at my eyelashes and stabbed at my stinging eyes. That's when everything began to reel. The sea carried up a thick, fiery breath. It seemed to me as if the sky split open from one end to the other to rain down fire. My whole being tensed and I squeezed my hand around the revolver. The trigger gave; I felt the smooth underside of the butt; and there, in that noise, sharp and deafening at the same time, is where it all started. I shook off the sweat and sun. I knew that I had shattered the harmony of the day, the exceptional silence of a beach where I'd been happy. Then I fired four more times at the motionless body where the bullets lodged without leaving a trace. And it was like knocking four quick times on the door of unhappiness.

1 **dazzling spear** まぶしい槍　2 **scorching blade** 焼けつくような刃　**slashed** 切りつけた　**eyelashes** まつげ　**stabbed** 突き刺した　3 **stinging** ひりひり痛む　**reel** くるくる回る　4 **thick, fiery breath** 重い、炎のような息　5 **from one end to the other** 端から端まで　**to rain down fire** 雨のように日光を降らせる　6 **My whole being** 全身　**tensed** 緊張した、こわばった　7 **The trigger gave** 引き金が引かれた　8 **butt** ピストルの握りの部分　**there...**（there は次の行の is where... に続く）　**in that noise, sharp and deafening at the same time** その、鋭く鼓膜の破れそうな音の中で　9 **is where it all started** すべてが始まったのだった　10 **shook off the sweat and sun** 汗と日の光を振り払った　13 **lodged** めりこんだ　14 **without leaving a trace** 被弾した跡がみえない

PART TWO

1

Right after my arrest I was questioned several times, but it was just so they could find out who I was, which didn't take long. The first time, at the police station, nobody seemed very interested in my case. A week later, however, the examining magistrate looked me over with curiosity. But to get things started he simply asked my name and address, my occupation, the date and place of my birth. Then he wanted to know if I had hired an attorney. I admitted I hadn't and inquired whether it was really necessary to have one. "Why do you ask?" he said. I said I thought my case was pretty simple. He smiled and said, "That's your opinion. But the law is the law. If you don't hire an attorney yourself, the court will appoint one." I thought it was very convenient that the court should take care of those details. I told him so. He agreed with me and concluded that it was a good law.

At first, I didn't take him seriously. I was led into a curtained room; there was a single lamp on his desk which was shining on a chair where he had me sit while he remained standing in the shadows. I had read descriptions of scenes like this in books and it all seemed like a game to me. After our conversation, though, I looked at him and saw a tall, fine-featured man with deep-set blue eyes, a long gray moustache, and lots of thick, almost white hair. He struck me as being very reasonable and, overall, quite pleasant, despite a nervous tic which made his mouth twitch now and then. On my way out I was

3 **Right after** すぐあと 4 **it was just so** それは〜するためだった 7 **examining magistrate** 予審判事 **looked me over** しげしげとみた、調べた 9 **occupation** 職業 11 **attorney** 弁護士 **inquired** 質問した 12 **one** = an attorney 16 **appoint** 指名する 17 **those details** そういう細々したこと 18 **concluded** 締めくくった

21 **had me sit** 私を腰かけさせた 22 **descriptions of scenes** こんな情景の描写 25 **fine-featured** 端整な作りの顔 **deep-set** 奥目 27 **struck me as**（as 以下のように）私に印象づけた 28 **overall** 全体として **despite** 〜にもかかわらず 29 **twitch** ゆがむ **On my way out** 私がそこを出るとき

even going to shake his hand, but just in time, I remembered that I had killed a man.

The next day a lawyer came to see me at the prison. He was short and chubby, quite young, his hair carefully slicked back. Despite the heat (I was in my shirt sleeves), he had on a dark suit, a wing collar, and an odd-looking tie with broad black and white stripes. He put the briefcase he was carrying down on my bed, introduced himself, and said he had gone over my file. My case was a tricky one, but he had no doubts we'd win, if I trusted him. I thanked him and he said, "Let's get down to business."

He sat down on the bed and explained to me that there had been some investigations into my private life. It had been learned that my mother had died recently at the home. Inquiries had then been made in Marengo. The investigators had learned that I had "shown insensitivity" the day of Maman's funeral. "You understand," my lawyer said, "it's a little embarrassing for me to have to ask you this. But it's very important. And it will be a strong argument for the prosecution if I can't come up with some answers." He wanted me to help him. He asked if I had felt any sadness that day. The question caught me by surprise and it seemed to me that I would have been very embarrassed if I'd had to ask it. Nevertheless I answered that I had pretty much lost the habit of analyzing myself and that it was hard for me to tell him what he wanted to know. I probably did love Maman, but that didn't mean anything. At one time

1 **just in time** ちょうど間に合った
3 **lawyer** 弁護士　4 **chubby** ずんぐりした　5 **slicked back** 後ろになでつけてある　**shirt sleeves** シャツの袖　6 **dark suit** 黒のスーツ　**wing collar** ウイングカラー（正装用の白いシャツの立ち襟）　7 **odd-looking** 風変わりな　**stripes** 縞模様　8 **briefcase** ブリーフケース　9 **had gone over my file** 私の書類に目を通した　10 **tricky** 難しい、微妙な　11 **Let's get down to business** 要件に入りましょう
17 **investigators** 取り調べをした人々　**insensitivity** 無神経さ、冷酷さ　19 **embarrassing** やりづらい　21 **prosecution** 検察側　22 **come up with** みつける、考えだす　24 **caught me by surprise** 私を驚かせた　27 **the habit of analyzing myself** 自分を分析する習慣　29 **At one time or another** いつとはっきりはいえないが

or another all normal people have wished their loved ones were dead. Here the lawyer interrupted me and he seemed very upset. He made me promise I wouldn't say that at my hearing or in front of the examining magistrate. I explained to him, however, that my nature was such that my physical needs often got in the way of my feelings. The day I buried Maman, I was very tired and sleepy, so much so that I wasn't really aware of what was going on. What I can say for certain is that I would rather Maman hadn't died. But my lawyer didn't seem satisfied. He said, "That's not enough."

He thought for a minute. He asked me if he could say that that day I had held back my natural feelings. I said, "No, because it's not true." He gave me a strange look, as if he found me slightly disgusting. He told me in an almost snide way that in any case the director and the staff of the home would be called as witnesses and that "things could get very nasty" for me. I pointed out to him that none of this had anything to do with my case, but all he said was that it was obvious I had never had any dealings with the law.

He left, looking angry. I wished I could have made him stay, to explain that I wanted things between us to be good, not so that he'd defend me better but, if I can put it this way, good in a natural way. Mostly, I could tell, I made him feel uncomfortable. He didn't understand me, and he was sort of holding it against me. I felt the urge to reassure him that I was like everybody else, just like everybody else. But really there wasn't much

2 **interrupted me** 私をさえぎった 3 **upset** あわてている 4 **hearing** 尋問 6 **my physical needs** 肉体的な要求 **got in the way of my feelings** 感情の邪魔をする 9 **What I can say for certain** 自分がまちがいなくいえることは

13 **had held back** 抑えた 15 **found me slightly disgusting** 私をちょっといやなやつだと思った 16 **snide** 悪意のある 18 **nasty** 不利 21 **dealings with the law** 法律的なこと、(裁判)に関わること

24 **not so that he'd defend me better but, if I can put it this way, good in a natural way** (not...but の構文。if I can put it this way「こういっていいのであれば、いわせてもらえば」は挿入句) 彼が私をうまく弁護できるためにではなく、こういっていいのであればだが、自然な形でちゃんと弁護してもらいたいからだ 25 **Mostly** 全体的に 26 **tell** わかる 27 **holding it against me** 私に悪意を抱く 28 **reassure** 安心させる 29 **there wasn't much point** あまり役に立たないことだった

point, and I gave up the idea out of laziness.

Shortly after that, I was taken before the examining magistrate again. It was two o'clock in the afternoon, and this time his office was filled with sunlight barely softened by a flimsy curtain. It was very hot. He had me sit down and very politely informed me that, "due to unforeseen circumstances," my lawyer had been unable to come. But I had the right to remain silent and to wait for my lawyer's counsel. I said that I could answer for myself. He pressed a button on the table. A young clerk came in and sat down right behind me.

The two of us leaned back in our chairs. The examination began. He started out by saying that people were describing me as a taciturn and withdrawn person and he wanted to know what I thought. I answered, "It's just that I don't have much to say. So I keep quiet." He smiled the way he had the first time, agreed that that was the best reason of all, and added, "Besides, it's not important." Then he looked at me without saying anything, leaned forward rather abruptly, and said very quickly, "What interests me is you." I didn't really understand what he meant by that, so I didn't respond. "There are one or two things," he added, "that I don't quite understand. I'm sure you'll help me clear them up." I said it was all pretty simple. He pressed me to go back over that day. I went back over what I had already told him: Raymond, the beach, the swim, the quarrel, then back to the beach, the little spring, the sun, and the five shots from the revolver. After each sentence he

1 **out of laziness** 怠慢から、面倒臭いので
4 **sunlight barely softened by a flimsy curtain** 薄いカーテンではろくにやわらげられない太陽の光　6 **informed** 告げた　**due to** ～のために　7 **unforeseen circumstances** 不測の事態　8 **right** 権利　9 **counsel** 相談
12 **leaned back** 後ろにもたれた　14 **taciturn** 口数の少ない　**withdrawn** 内向的な　17 **the way he had the first time** 最初のときにしたように　20 **leaned forward** 身を乗り出した　**abruptly** いきなり　22 **by that** その言葉（What interests me is you.）　25 **pressed** うながした　**go back over that day** あの日のことを思い出して話す

would say, "Fine, fine." When I got to the body lying there, he nodded and said, "Good." But I was tired of repeating the same story over and over. It seemed as if I had never talked so much in my life.

After a short silence, he stood up and told me that he wanted to help me, that I interested him, and that, with God's help, he would do something for me. But first he wanted to ask me a few more questions. Without working up to it, he asked if I loved Maman. I said, "Yes, the same as anyone," and the clerk, who up to then had been typing steadily, must have hit the wrong key, because he lost his place and had to go back. Again without any apparent logic, the magistrate then asked if I had fired all five shots at once. I thought for a minute and explained that at first I had fired a single shot and then, a few seconds later, the other four. Then he said, "Why did you pause between the first and second shot?" Once again I could see the red sand and feel the burning of the sun on my forehead. But this time I didn't answer. In the silence that followed, the magistrate seemed to be getting fidgety. He sat down, ran his fingers through his hair, put his elbows on his desk, and leaned toward me slightly with a strange look on his face. "Why, why did you shoot at a body that was on the ground?" Once again I didn't know how to answer. The magistrate ran his hands across his forehead and repeated his question with a slightly different tone in his voice. "Why? You must tell me. Why?" Still I didn't say anything.

Suddenly he stood up, strode over to a far corner of

5 **told** told の内容は2つ（① that he... と ② that, with） 8 **Without working up to it** おだやかな調子で 10 **clerk** 書記 11 **hit the wrong key** タイプライターのキーを打ち間違えた 12 **lost his place** あわてた 13 **without any apparent logic** それらしい理由もなく（これといって論理的なつながりもなく） 21 **fidgety** いらいらする 25 **ran his hands across his forehead** 両手で額をなでた
29 **strode** 大股で歩いた

his office, and pulled out a drawer in a file cabinet. He took out a silver crucifix which he brandished as he came toward me. And in a completely different, almost cracked voice, he shouted, "Do you know what this is?" I said, "Yes, of course." Speaking very quickly and passionately, he told me that he believed in God, that it was his conviction that no man was so guilty that God would not forgive him, but in order for that to happen a man must repent and in so doing become like a child whose heart is open and ready to embrace all. He was leaning all the way over the table. He was waving his crucifix almost directly over my head. To tell the truth, I had found it very hard to follow his reasoning, first because I was hot and there were big flies in his office that kept landing on my face, and also because he was scaring me a little. At the same time I knew that that was ridiculous because, after all, I was the criminal. He went on anyway. I vaguely understood that to his mind there was just one thing that wasn't clear in my confession, the fact that I had hesitated before I fired my second shot. The rest was fine, but that part he couldn't understand.

I was about to tell him he was wrong to dwell on it, because it really didn't matter. But he cut me off and urged me one last time, drawing himself up to his full height and asking me if I believed in God. I said no. He sat down indignantly. He said it was impossible; all men believed in God, even those who turn their backs on him. That was his belief, and if he were ever to doubt it, his life would become meaningless. "Do you want my

1 **drawer** 引出し　2 **crucifix** 十字架　**brandished** 振った 4 **cracked** しゃがれた、割れた　7 **conviction** 確信　**no man was so guilty that God would not forgive him** だれも、神が許さないほどの罪を犯すことはない（神はどんな罪をも許す） 8 **in order for that to happen** そうなるためには（許しを得るためには）　9 **repent** 悔い改める　10 **leaning all the way over the table** テーブルの上に大きく身を乗りだした　11 **waving** 振る　13 **follow his reasoning** 彼の説明についていく　14 **flies** 書類　15 **scaring** 怖がらせる　21 **The rest was fine** ほかの部分はそれでよかった

22 **to dwell on it** そのことに固執する、こだわる　23 **cut me off** 私を黙らせた　24 **urged me one last time** 最後にもう一度、うながした　**drawing himself up to his full height** 背筋をすっと伸ばして　26 **indignantly** 腹立たしげに　28 **if he were ever to doubt it** もしそれ（彼の信念）を疑うことになったら

life to be meaningless?" he shouted. As far as I could see, it didn't have anything to do with me, and I told him so. But from across the table he had already thrust the crucifix in my face and was screaming irrationally, "I am a Christian. I ask Him to forgive you your sins. How can you not believe that He suffered for you?" I was struck by how sincere he seemed, but I had had enough. It was getting hotter and hotter. As always, whenever I want to get rid of someone I'm not really listening to, I made it appear as if I agreed. To my surprise, he acted triumphant. "You see, you see!" he said. "You do believe, don't you, and you're going to place your trust in Him, aren't you?" Obviously, I again said no. He fell back in his chair.

He seemed to be very tired. He didn't say anything for a minute while the typewriter, which hadn't let up the whole time, was still tapping out the last few sentences. Then he looked at me closely and with a little sadness in his face. In a low voice he said, "I have never seen a soul as hardened as yours. The criminals who have come before me have always wept at the sight of this image of suffering." I was about to say that that was precisely because they were criminals. But then I realized that I was one too. It was an idea I couldn't get used to. Then the judge stood up, as if to give me the signal that the examination was over. He simply asked, in the same weary tone, if I was sorry for what I had done. I thought about it for a minute and said that more than sorry I felt kind of annoyed. I got the impression

2 **it didn't have anything to do with me** それは私には関係が無かった　4 **irrationally** 感情的に　5 **forgive you your sins** あなたにあなたの罪を許す　6 **He suffered** 神は受難なさった　7 **sincere** 誠実　**I had had enough** がまんできなかった　10 **I made it appear as if I agreed** 私は相手に同意したような振りをした　11 **triumphant** 勝ちほこった
16 **hadn't let up the whole time** しじゅう止まることがなかった　20 **hardened** 頑なな　**yours** your soul　22 **this image of suffering** この受難の像（十字架のキリスト像）　24 **It was an idea I couldn't get used to** それ（自分が罪人であるということ）は、私が慣れることのできない考えだった　25 **the judge**（予審）判事　27 **weary** 疲れた　29 **kind of annoyed** いささか当惑した

he didn't understand. But that was as far as things went that day.

After that, I saw a lot of the magistrate, except that my lawyer was with me each time. But it was just a matter of clarifying certain things in my previous statements. Or else the magistrate would discuss the charges with my lawyer. But on those occasions they never really paid much attention to me. Anyway, the tone of the questioning gradually changed. The magistrate seemed to have lost interest in me and to have come to some sort of decision about my case. He didn't talk to me about God anymore, and I never saw him as worked up as he was that first day. The result was that our discussions became more cordial. A few questions, a brief conversation with my lawyer, and the examinations were over. As the magistrate put it, my case was taking its course. And then sometimes, when the conversation was of a more general nature, I would be included. I started to breathe more freely. No one, in any of these meetings, was rough with me. Everything was so natural, so well handled, and so calmly acted out that I had the ridiculous impression of being "one of the family." And I can say that at the end of the eleven months that this investigation lasted, I was almost surprised that I had ever enjoyed anything other than those rare moments when the judge would lead me to the door of his office, slap me on the shoulder, and say to me cordially, "That's all for today, Monsieur Antichrist." I would then be handed back over to the police.

1 **that was as far as things went that day** その日の尋問はそこまでだった
3 **saw a lot of** 何度も会った 5 **clarifying** 確認する 6 **charges** 告訴、告発 10 **have come to some sort of decision about my case** 私の件についてある程度の決定にいたった 12 **as worked up as he was that first day** 最初の日と同じくらいの熱意をみせる 14 **cordial** 親密な 16 **put it** いった **taking its course** お決まりの手順をとる 18 **general nature** 一般的な種類 **included** 話に参加させられた 20 **rough with me** 私に対してひどい態度を取る 21 **well handled** うまく処理された **acted out** 行動に移された 24 **lasted** 続いた 25 **anything other than** = anything but、〜以外すべて 27 **cordially** やさしく 28 **That's all for today** 今日はこれで終わりです **Antichrist** 反キリスト

2

There are some things I've never liked talking about. A few days after I entered prison, I realized that I wouldn't like talking about this part of my life.

Later on, though, I no longer saw any point to my reluctance. In fact, I wasn't really in prison those first few days: I was sort of waiting for something to happen. It was only after Marie's first and last visit that it all started. From the day I got her letter (she told me she would no longer be allowed to come, because she wasn't my wife), from that day on I felt that I was at home in my cell and that my life was coming to a standstill there. The day of my arrest I was first put in a room where there were already several other prisoners, most of them Arabs. They laughed when they saw me. Then they asked me what I was in for. I said I'd killed an Arab and they were all silent. A few minutes later, it got dark. They showed me how to fix the mat I was supposed to sleep on. One end could be rolled up to make a pillow. All night I felt bugs crawling over my face. A few days later I was put in a cell by myself, where I slept on wooden boards suspended from the wall. I had a bucket for a toilet and a tin washbasin. The prison was on the heights above the town, and through a small window I could see the sea. One day as I was gripping the bars, my face straining toward the light, a guard came in and told me I had a visitor. I thought it must be Marie. It was.

6 **Later on** その後、そのうちに **any point to my reluctance**（刑務所でのことについて話すのを）いやがる理由 9 **It was only after Marie's first and last visit that**（It was...that の強調構文）マリーの最初にして最後の面会のあと、すべては始まったのだ 12 **was at home in my cell** 独房のなかは居心地がよかった 14 **standstill** 静止状態 19 **how to fix the mat** マットの使いかた、敷きかた 21 **bugs** 虫 **crawling** はう 23 **suspended from the wall**（ロープか鎖で）壁から吊ってある 24 **tin wash-basin** ブリキの洗面器 25 **the heights** 高台 26 **gripping the bars** 格子をつかむ 27 **straining toward the light** せいいっぱい光のほうに突きだす

To get to the visiting room I went down a long corridor, then down some stairs and, finally, another corridor. I walked into a very large room brightened by a huge bay window. The room was divided into three sections by two large grates that ran the length of the room. Between the two grates was a space of eight to ten meters which separated the visitors from the prisoners. I spotted Marie standing at the opposite end of the room with her striped dress and her sun-tanned face. On my side of the room there were about ten prisoners, most of them Arabs. Marie was surrounded by Moorish women and found herself between two visitors: a little, thin-lipped old woman dressed in black and a fat, bareheaded woman who was talking at the top of her voice and making lots of gestures. Because of the distance between the grates, the visitors and the prisoners were forced to speak very loud. When I walked in, the sound of the voices echoing off the room's high, bare walls and the harsh light pouring out of the sky onto tile windows and spilling into the room brought on a kind of dizziness. My cell was quieter and darker. It took me a few seconds to adjust. But eventually I could see each face clearly, distinctly in the bright light. I noticed there was a guard sitting at the far end of the passage between the two grates. Most of the Arab prisoners and their families had squatted down facing each other. They weren't shouting. Despite the commotion, they were managing to make themselves heard by talking in very low voices. Their subdued murmuring, coming from

1 **visiting room** 面会室 **corridor** 廊下 4 **bay window** 張り出し窓 5 **ran the length of the room** 部屋を走っていた（区切っていた） 8 **spotted** みつけた 9 **sun-tanned** 日焼けした 11 **Moorish women** ムーア人の女たち 14 **bareheaded** 帽子をかぶっていない **at the top of her voice** 声を張りあげて 17 **the sound…dizziness**（① the sound of the voices echoing off the room's high, bare walls「部屋の高くて、むきだしの壁に反響する声」と② the harsh light pouring out of the sky onto tile windows and spilling into the room「タイル枠の窓を通って空から降りそそぎ、部屋の中にあふれるまぶしい光」が、brought on a kind of dizziness「ある種のめまいを催させた」） 22 **adjust** 慣れる 26 **squatted down** しゃがんでいた 27 **commotion** 騒々しさ 28 **make themselves heard** 自分の話を伝える 29 **subdued** 抑えた **murmuring** 小声 **from lower down** 下から響いてくる

lower down, formed a kind of bass accompaniment to the conversations crossing above their heads. I took all this in very quickly as I made my way toward Marie. Already pressed up against the grate, she was smiling her best smile for me. I thought she looked very beautiful, but I didn't know how to tell her.

"Well?" she called across to me. "Well, here I am."

"Are you all right? Do you have everything you want?"

"Yes, everything."

We stopped talking and Marie went on smiling. The fat woman yelled to the man next to me, her husband probably, a tall blond guy with an honest face. It was the continuation of a conversation already under way.

"Jeanne wouldn't take him," she shouted as loudly as she could. "Uh-huh," said the man. "I told her you'd take him back when you get out, but she wouldn't take him."

Then it was Marie's turn to shout, that Raymond sent his regards, and I said, "Thanks." But my voice was drowned out by the man next to me, who asked, "Is he all right?" His wife laughed and said, "He's never been better." The man on my left, a small young man with delicate hands, wasn't saying anything. I noticed that he was across from the little old lady and that they were staring intently at each other. But I didn't have time to watch them any longer, because Marie shouted to me that I had to have hope. I said, "Yes." I was looking at her as she said it and I wanted to squeeze her shoulders through her dress. I wanted to feel the thin material and

1 **bass accompaniment** 低音の伴奏　2 **took all this in** それらのことすべてを見てとった　4 **pressed up against the grate** 格子に体を押しつけている、張りついている
13 **continuation** 続き　**already under way** すでに行われていた
14 **Jeanne** ジャンヌ　**take him** 彼を引き受ける　16 **take him back** 彼を引き取る
18 **sent his regards** よろしくといっていた　19 **was drowned out** かき消された　21 **never been better** これまでになかったほどいい　23 **delicate** きゃしゃな　25 **intently** 真剣に
28 **squeeze her shoulders** 肩を抱きしめる　29 **through her dress** ワンピースの上から　**the thin material** 薄い素材（ワンピースの布）

I didn't really know what else I had to hope for other than that. But that was probably what Marie meant, because she was still smiling. All I could see was the sparkle of her teeth and the little folds of her eyes. She shouted again, "You'll get out and we'll get married!" I answered, "You think so?" but it was mainly just to say something. Then very quickly and still in a very loud voice she said yes, that I would be acquitted and that we would go swimming again. But the other woman took her turn to shout and said that she had left a basket at the clerk's office. She was listing all the things she had put in it, to make sure they were all there, because they cost a lot of money. The young man and his mother were still staring at each other. The murmuring of the Arabs continued below us. Outside, the light seemed to surge up over the bay window.

I was feeling a little sick and I'd have liked to leave. The noise was getting painful. But on the other hand, I wanted to make the most of Marie's being there. I don't know how much time went by. Marie told me about her job and she never stopped smiling. The murmuring, the shouting, and the conversations were crossing back and forth. The only oasis of silence was next to me where the small young man and the old woman were gazing at each other. One by one the Arabs were taken away. Almost everyone stopped talking as soon as the first one left. The little old woman moved closer to the bars, and at the same moment a guard motioned to her son. He said "Goodbye, Maman," and she reached between two

1 **what else I had to hope for other than that** それ以外、何を望むだろう 2 **what Marie meant** マリーのいいたかったこと 4 **sparkle** 輝き **folds** シワ 6 **it was mainly just to say something** それは（You think so? といったのは）主に、何かいわなくてはと思ったからだった 8 **be acquitted** 釈放される 10 **took her turn to shout** 彼女が叫ぶ番だった 11 **clerk's office** 書記のオフィス 15 **below us** 私たちの下のほうで 16 **surge up** 押し寄せてくる
17 **sick** 吐き気 19 **make the most of** 最大限に利用する、楽しむ 23 **oasis** オアシス 25 **were taken away** 連れて行かれた 28 **motioned** 身ぶりで合図した

bars to give him a long, slow little wave.

She left just as another man came in, hat in hand, and took her place. Another prisoner was brought in and they talked excitedly, but softly, because the room had once again grown quiet. They came for the man on my right, and his wife said to him without lowering her voice, as if she hadn't noticed there was no need to shout anymore, "Take care of yourself and be careful." Then it was my turn. Marie threw me a kiss. I looked back before disappearing. She hadn't moved and her face was still pressed against the bars with the same sad, forced smile on it.

Shortly after that was when she wrote to me. And the things I've never liked talking about began. Anyway, I shouldn't exaggerate, and it was easier for me than for others. When I was first imprisoned, the hardest thing was that my thoughts were still those of a free man. For example, I would suddenly have the urge to be on a beach and to walk down to the water. As I imagined the sound of the first waves under my feet, my body entering the water and the sense of relief it would give me, all of a sudden I would feel just how closed in I was by the walls of my cell. But that only lasted a few months. Afterwards my only thoughts were those of a prisoner. I waited for the daily walk, which I took in the courtyard, or for a visit from my lawyer. The rest of the time I managed pretty well. At the time, I often thought that if I had had to live in the trunk of a dead tree, with nothing to do but look up at the sky flowering overhead, little by

1 **wave**（さようならと）手を振る仕草
3 **took her place** 彼女と交替した　5 **They came for the man on my right** 彼ら（守衛）が私の右側の男を連れにやってきた
9 **my turn** 私の番
13 **the things I've never liked talking about began** 私の絶対に話したくないことが始まった　15 **it was easier for me than for others** ほかの人よりは私のほうがそれ（話さないこと）は得意だ　22 **closed in** 閉じこめられている、取り囲まれている
27 **managed pretty well** かなりうまくやっていた　28 **trunk of a dead tree** 枯木の幹　29 **the sky flowering overhead** 頭上に花開いているようにみえる空

little I would have gotten used to it. I would have waited for birds to fly by or clouds to mingle, just as here I waited to see my lawyer's ties and just as, in another world, I used to wait patiently until Saturday to hold Marie's body in my arms. Now, as I think back on it, I wasn't in a hollow tree trunk. There were others worse off than me. Anyway, it was one of Maman's ideas, and she often repeated it, that after a while you could get used to anything.

Besides, I usually didn't take things so far. The first months were hard. But in fact the effort I had to make helped pass the time. For example, I was tormented by my desire for a woman. It was only natural; I was young. I never thought specifically of Marie. But I thought so much about a woman, about women, about all the ones I had known, about all the circumstances in which I had enjoyed them, that my cell would be filled with their faces and crowded with my desires. In one sense, it threw me off balance. But in another, it killed time. I had ended up making friends with the head guard, who used to make the rounds with the kitchen hands at mealtime. He's the one who first talked to me about women. He told me it was the first thing the others complained about. I told him it was the same for me and that I thought it was unfair treatment. "But," he said, "that's exactly why you're in prison." "What do you mean that's why?" "Well, yes—freedom, that's why. They've taken away your freedom." I'd never thought about that. I agreed. "It's true," I said. "Otherwise,

2 **clouds to mingle** 雲が混じり合う 5 **I wasn't in a hollow tree trunk** 私はうつろな木の幹の中にいるのではなかった
6 **worse off** 私よりも不幸な
10 **I usually didn't take things so far** 私は普通、物事をそこまで考えない 12 **pass the time** 時間を過ごす、つぶす 13 **desire for a woman** 女に対する欲望 16 **circumstances** 状態、状況 19 **threw me off balance** そのせいで私は（精神的な）バランスを失った **killed time** 時間をつぶしてくれた 20 **ended up** そのうち〜した **making friends with** 仲よくなる 21 **make the rounds** 回ってくる、巡回する **the kitchen hands** 給仕人 29 **Otherwise** そうでなければ

what would be the punishment?" "Right. You see, you understand these things. The rest of them don't. But they just end up doing it by themselves." The guard left after that.

There were the cigarettes, too. When I entered prison, they took away my belt, my shoelaces, my tie, and everything I had in my pockets, my cigarettes in particular. Once I was in my cell, I asked to have them back. But I was told I wasn't allowed. The first few days were really rough. That may be the thing that was hardest for me. I would suck on chips of wood that I broke off my bed planks. I walked around nauseated all day long. I couldn't understand why they had taken them away when they didn't hurt anybody. Later on I realized that that too was part of the punishment. But by then I had gotten used to not smoking and it wasn't a punishment anymore.

Apart from these annoyances, I wasn't too unhappy. Once again the main problem was killing time. Eventually, once I learned how to remember things, I wasn't bored at all. Sometimes I would get to thinking about my room, and in my imagination I would start at one corner and circle the room, mentally noting everything there was on the way. At first it didn't take long. But every time I started over, it took a little longer. I would remember every piece of furniture; and on every piece of furniture, every object; and of every object, all the details; and of the details themselves—a flake, a crack, or a chipped edge—the color and the texture. At the same

3 **doing it by themselves** 自分で処理する

6 **shoelaces** 靴紐　7 **in particular** とくに　11 **suck on chips of wood** 木切れをしゃぶる　12 **planks** 板　**nauseated** 吐き気を覚えながら　14 **when they didn't hurt anybody** だれの害になるわけでもないのに

18 **annoyances** 不満　20 **remember** 覚える　23 **mentally** 頭の中で　**noting** 認識していく　24 **on the way**（部屋を一周する）途中の　26 **on every piece of furniture, every object** ひとつひとつの家具については、それにはどんな物が置かれていたか　27 **of every object, all the details** ひとつひとつの物については、その細かい特徴をすべて　28 **of the details themselves** 細かい特徴そのものについては　**a flake** はげた部分　**a crack** ひび割れ　29 **a chipped edge** 欠けた角

time I would try not to lose the thread of my inventory, to make a complete list, so that after a few weeks I could spend hours just enumerating the things that were in my room. And the more I thought about it, the more I dug out of my memory things I had overlooked or forgotten. I realized then that a man who had lived only one day could easily live for a hundred years in prison. He would have enough memories to keep him from being bored. In a way, it was an advantage.

Then there was sleep. At first, I didn't sleep well at night and not at all during the day. Little by little, my nights got better and I was able to sleep during the day, too. In fact, during the last few months I've been sleeping sixteen to eighteen hours a day. That would leave me six hours to kill with meals, nature's call, my memories, and the story about the Czechoslovakian.

Between my straw mattress and the bed planks, I had actually found an old scrap of newspaper, yellow and transparent, half-stuck to the canvas. On it was a news story, the first part of which was missing, but which must have taken place in Czechoslovakia. A man had left a Czech village to seek his fortune. Twenty-five years later, and now rich, he had returned with a wife and a child. His mother was running a hotel with his sister in the village where he'd been born. In order to surprise them, he had left his wife and child at another hotel and gone to see his mother, who didn't recognize him when he walked in. As a joke he'd had the idea of taking a room. He had shown off his money. During the

1 **not to lose the thread of my inventory** 家具などの目録を忘れないように 3 **enumerating** 列挙する 5 **dug out of my memory things I had overlooked or forgotten** 記憶の中から、見逃したり忘れていた物を掘りだす 6 **a man who had lived only one day could easily live for a hundred years in prison** たった1日でも（外の世界で）生活をした人間は百年でも刑務所で楽に暮らすことができる 8 **keep him from being bored** 自分を退屈から遠ざける 9 **advantage** 利点

15 **nature's call** 生理的な欲求、用便 16 **the story about the Czechoslovakian** チェコスロバキア人についての話

17 **straw mattress** 麦ワラのマットレス 18 **scrap** 切り抜き 19 **transparent** 向こうが透けている **half-stuck to the canvas** マットレスのキャンバス地になかば張りついていた 21 **have taken place** 起こった 22 **seek his fortune** ひと財産こしらえに 29 **taking a room** 部屋を借りる **had shown off** 自慢そうにみせた

night his mother and his sister had beaten him to death with a hammer in order to rob him and had thrown his body in the river. The next morning the wife had come to the hotel and, without knowing it, gave away the traveler's identity. The mother hanged herself. The sister threw herself down a well. I must have read that story a thousand times. On the one hand it wasn't very likely. On the other, it was perfectly natural. Anyway, I thought the traveler pretty much deserved what he got and that you should never play games.

So, with all the sleep, my memories, reading my crime story, and the alternation of light and darkness, time passed. Of course I had read that eventually you wind up losing track of time in prison. But it hadn't meant much to me when I'd read it. I hadn't understood how days could be both long and short at the same time: long to live through, maybe, but so drawn out that they ended up flowing into one another. They lost their names. Only the words "yesterday" and "tomorrow" still had any meaning for me.

One day when the guard told me that I'd been in for five months, I believed it, but I didn't understand it. For me it was one and the same unending day that was unfolding in my cell and the same thing I was trying to do. That day, after the guard had left, I looked at myself in my tin plate. My reflection seemed to remain serious even though I was trying to smile at it. I moved the plate around in front of me. I smiled and it still had the same sad, stern expression. It was near the end of the day,

4 **gave away the traveler's identity** 旅人がだれかを明かした 5 **hanged herself** 首を吊った 6 **a well** 井戸 7 **wasn't very likely** あまりありそうなことではない 9 **deserved what he got** したことの報いを受けた、身から出た錆 10 **play games** ふざける

11 **with...darkness**（①the sleep、②my memories、③reading my crime story、④the alternation of light and darkness などで） 13 **time passed** 時間が過ぎていった **you**（一般人称） 14 **wind up** ～の状態になってしまう **losing track of time** 時間の感覚を失う 17 **long to live through**（単調な毎日を）生きていくには長い **drawn out** 引き延ばされて 18 **flowing into one another** 互いに流れこんでしまう、入り混じってしまう

23 **it was one and the same unending day that was unfolding in my cell**（it was...that の強調構文）終わることのないまさに同じ1日が独房のなかで展開した 24 **the same thing I was trying to do** 同じことをしていた 25 **looked at myself in my tin plate** ブリキの皿に自分を映してみた 26 **reflection** 皿に映った自分の顔 29 **stern** いかめしい、むっつりした

the time of day I don't like talking about, that nameless hour when the sounds of evening would rise up from every floor of the prison in a cortege of silence. I moved closer to the window, and in the last light of day I gazed at my reflection one more time. It was still serious—and what was surprising about that, since at that moment I was too? But at the same time, and for the first time in months, I distinctly heard the sound of my own voice. I recognized it as the same one that had been ringing in my ears for many long days, and I realized that all that time I had been talking to myself. Then I remembered what the nurse at Maman's funeral said. No, there was no way out, and no one can imagine what nights in prison are like.

1 **nameless** 名前のない　3 **in a cortege of silence** 沈黙の行列　6 **what was surprising about that** そのことで何を驚くことがあるだろう　**I was too?** (I was serious too?)　10 **for many long days** 長いあいだずっと　12 **there was no way out** 逃げ道はなかった

3

But I can honestly say that the time from summer to summer went very quickly. And I knew as soon as the weather turned hot that something new was in store for me. My case was set down for the last session of the Court of Assizes, and that session was due to end some time in June. The trial opened with the sun glaring outside. My lawyer had assured me that it wouldn't last more than two or three days. "Besides," he had added, "the court will be pressed for time. Yours isn't the most important case of the session. Right after you, there's a parricide coming up."

They came for me at seven-thirty in the morning and I was driven to the courthouse in the prison van. The two policemen took me into a small room that smelled of darkness. We waited, seated near a door through which we could hear voices, shouts, chairs being dragged across the floor, and a lot of commotion which made me think of those neighborhood fêtes when the hall is cleared for dancing after the concert. The policemen told me we had to wait for the judges and one of them offered me a cigarette, which I turned down. Shortly after that he asked me if I had the "jitters." I said no—and that, in a way, I was even interested in seeing a trial. I'd never had the chance before. "Yeah," said the other policeman, "but it gets a little boring after a while."

A short time later a small bell rang in the room. Then they took my handcuffs off. They opened the door and

5 **in store** 待ちかまえている　6 **was set down**　決められていた　**for the last session** 最後の会期　7 **Court of Assizes** 巡回裁判　8 **trial** 裁判　11 **pressed for time** 時間がない　13 **parricide** 親殺し

16 **smelled of darkness** 闇のにおいがした　18 **chairs being dragged across the floor** 床の上を引きずられる椅子　19 **commotion** 騒々しさ　20 **neighborhood fêtes** 近所で行われた祭　21 **cleared**（椅子などを）片づける　23 **turned down** 断った　24 **jitters** 不安　29 **handcuffs** 手錠

led me into the dock. The room was packed. Despite the blinds, the sun filtered through in places and the air was already stifling. They hadn't opened the windows. I sat down with the policemen standing on either side of me. It was then that I noticed a row of faces in front of me. They were all looking at me: I realized that they were the jury. But I can't say what distinguished one from another. I had just one impression: I was sitting across from a row of seats on a streetcar and all these anonymous passengers were looking over the new arrival to see if they could find something funny about him. I knew it was a silly idea since it wasn't anything funny they were after but a crime. There isn't much difference, though—in any case that was the idea that came to me.

I was feeling a little dizzy too, with all those people in that stuffy room. I looked around the courtroom again but I couldn't make out a single face. I think that at first I hadn't realized that all those people were crowding in to see me. Usually people didn't pay much attention to me. It took some doing on my part to understand that I was the cause of all the excitement. I said to the policeman, "Some crowd!" He told me it was because of the press and he pointed to a group of men at a table just below the jury box. He said, "That's them." I asked, "Who?" and he repeated, "The press." He knew one of the reporters, who just then spotted him and was making his way toward us. He was an older, friendly man with a twisted little grin on his face. He gave the policeman a warm handshake. I noticed then that everyone was

1 **dock** 被告席 **packed** 人でいっぱいだった 2 **filtered through in places** あちこちに射しこんでいた 3 **stifling** 息苦しい 5 **It was then that**（It was...thatの強調構文） 7 **jury** 陪審員 **I can't say what distinguished one from another** ひとりひとり見分ける特徴がわからなかった 9 **anonymous** だれだかわからない 12 **since it wasn't anything funny they were after but a crime** なぜなら、彼らがさがしているのはおかしさではなく罪なのだから 14 **in any case** どうであれ **that was the idea that came to me** そんな考えが浮かんできたのだった 15 **dizzy** めまい 16 **stuffy** 蒸し暑い、息の詰まる 17 **make out** 見分ける 20 **It took some doing** かなりの労力、努力を必要とした 22 **Some crowd!** ずいぶん人が多いですね 23 **press** 新聞 24 **jury box** 陪審席 27 **with a twisted little grin** ゆがんだ笑みをちょっと浮かべた

waving and exchanging greetings and talking, as if they were in a club where people are glad to find themselves among others from the same world. That is how I explained to myself the strange impression I had of being odd man out, a kind of intruder. Yet the reporter turned and spoke to me with a smile. He told me that he hoped everything would go well for me. I thanked him and he added, "You know, we've blown your case up a little. Summer is the slow season for the news. And your story and the parricide were the only ones worth bothering about." Then he pointed in the direction of the group he had just left, at a little man who looked like a fattened-up weasel. He told me that the man was a special correspondent for a Paris paper. "Actually, he didn't come because of you. But since they assigned him to cover the parricide trial, they asked him to send a dispatch about your case at the same time." And again I almost thanked him. But I thought that that would be ridiculous. He waved cordially, shyly, and left us. We waited a few more minutes.

My lawyer arrived, in his gown, surrounded by lots of colleagues. He walked over to the reporters and shook some hands. They joked and laughed and looked completely at ease, until the moment when the bell in the court rang. Everyone went back to his place. My lawyer walked over to me, shook my hand, and advised me to respond briefly to the questions that would be put to me, not to volunteer anything, and to leave the rest to him.

To my left I heard the sound of a chair being pulled

1 **waving** 手を振っている 2 **club** 社交場 5 **odd man out** のけ者、はみ出し者 **intruder** ちん入者 **Yet** しかし 8 **we've blown your case up a little** あなたの事件をちょっと大げさに取りあげました 9 **slow season** ネタがとぼしい季節 10 **worth bothering about** 取りあげるに足りる 12 **fattened-up weasel** 太ったイタチ 13 **correspondent** 記者 16 **dispatch** 電報 19 **cordially** 親しげに

27 **be put to me** 私に向けられる 28 **volunteer** 自分から申し出る、言い立てる **leave the rest to him** あとは彼にまかせる

out and I saw a tall, thin man dressed in red and wearing a pince-nez who was carefully folding his robe as he sat down. That was the prosecutor. A bailiff said, "All rise." At the same time two large fans started to whir. Three judges, two in black, the third in red, entered with files in hand and walked briskly to the rostrum which dominated the room. The man in the red gown sat on the chair in the middle, set his cap down in front of him, wiped his bald little head with a handkerchief, and announced that the court was now in session.

The reporters already had their pens in hand. They all had the same indifferent and somewhat snide look on their faces. One of them, however, much younger than the others, wearing gray flannels and a blue tie, had left his pen lying in front of him and was looking at me. All I could see in his slightly lopsided face were his two very bright eyes, which were examining me closely without betraying any definable emotion. And I had the odd impression of being watched by myself. Maybe it was for that reason, and also because I wasn't familiar with all the procedures, that I didn't quite understand everything that happened next: the drawing of lots for the jury; the questions put by the presiding judge to my lawyer, the prosecutor, and the jury (each time, the jurors' heads would all turn toward the bench at the same time); the quick reading of the indictment, in which I recognized names of people and places; and some more questions to my lawyer.

Anyway, the presiding judge said he was going to

2 **pince-nez** 鼻眼鏡 **carefully folding his robe** ていねいに法服を折って 3 **prosecutor** 検事 **bailiff** 廷吏（法廷の雑務を行う人） **All rise** 全員、起立 4 **fans** 扇風機 **whir** 音を立てて回る 6 **briskly** きびきびと **rostrum** 壇 9 **bald little head** はげた小さな頭

11 **reporters** 記者たち 12 **snide** ずるそうな 14 **flannels** フランネルの服 16 **lopsided** 不均衡な、バランスの悪い 17 **closely** しげしげと 18 **betraying any definable emotion** はっきりした感情を表に出す 19 **it was…all the procedures, that** (it was...that の強調構文) そういった理由のせいと、こういった手続に慣れていなかったせいもあって 22 **drawing of lots for the jury** 陪審員を抽選で決めること 23 **presiding judge** 裁判長 24 **jurors' heads** 陪審員の頭 25 **turn toward the bench** 判事席のほうを向く 26 **indictment** 起訴状

proceed with the calling of witnesses. The bailiff read off some names that caught my attention. In the middle of what until then had been a shapeless mass of spectators, I saw them stand up one by one, only to disappear again through a side door: the director and the caretaker from the home, old Thomas Pérez, Raymond, Masson, Salamano, and Marie. She waved to me, anxiously. I was still feeling surprised that I hadn't seen them before when Céleste, the last to be called, stood up. I recognized next to him the little woman from the restaurant, with her jacket and her stiff and determined manner. She was staring right at me. But I didn't have time to think about them, because the presiding judge started speaking. He said that the formal proceedings were about to begin and that he didn't think he needed to remind the public to remain silent. According to him, he was there to conduct in an impartial manner the proceedings of a case which he would consider objectively. The verdict returned by the jury would be taken in a spirit of justice, and, in any event, he would have the courtroom cleared at the slightest disturbance.

It was getting hotter, and I could see the people in the courtroom fanning themselves with newspapers, which made a continuous low rustling sound. The presiding judge gave a signal and the bailiff brought over three fans made of woven straw which the three judges started waving immediately.

My examination began right away. The presiding judge questioned me calmly and even, it seemed to me,

1 **proceed with the calling of witnesses** 証人の召喚に移る 3 **a shapeless mass of spectators** 傍聴人たちの形のない塊 7 **anxiously** 不安そうに 11 **with her jacket** あの上着を着て **stiff and determined manner** 堅苦しく、きっぱりとした態度 15 **remind the public to remain silent** 傍聴人たちに静粛にという 17 **in an impartial manner** 公平な方法で 18 **objectively** 客観的に **The verdict returned by the jury** 陪審員による判決 19 **be taken in a spirit of justice** 正義の精神にのっとってなされる 20 **in any event** いずれにしても **cleared at the slightest disturbance** 少しでも妨害や騒動があった場合は、傍聴人に出ていってもらう
24 **continuous** 絶え間ない **rustling** 新聞紙であおぐ音
26 **woven straw** 麦ワラを編んだもの

with a hint of cordiality. Once again he had me state my name, age, date and place of birth, and although it irritated me, I realized it was only natural, because it would be a very serious thing to try the wrong man. Then he reread the narrative of what I'd done, turning to me every few sentences to ask "Is that correct?" Each time I answered "Yes, Your Honor," as my lawyer had instructed me to do. It took a long time because the judge went into minute detail in his narrative. The reporters were writing the whole time. I was conscious of being watched by the youngest of them and by the little robot woman. Everyone on the row of streetcar seats was turned directly toward the judge, who coughed, leafed through his file, and turned toward me, fanning himself.

He told me that he now had to turn to some questions that might seem irrelevant to my case but might in fact have a significant bearing on it. I knew right away he was going to talk about Maman again, and at the same time I could feel how much it irritated me. He asked me why I had put Maman in the home. I answered that it was because I didn't have the money to have her looked after and cared for. He asked me if it had been hard on me, and I answered that Maman and I didn't expect anything from each other anymore, or from anyone else either, and that we had both gotten used to our new lives. The judge then said that he didn't want to dwell on this point, and he asked the prosecutor if he had any further questions.

The prosecutor had his back half-turned to me, and

1 **a hint of cordiality** ちょっとした親密さ **had me state** 私に述べさせた 3 **natural** 当然 4 **try the wrong man** ほかの人間を間違えて裁判にかける 5 **reread** 再読した **narrative** 証言 6 **every few sentences** 何文か読むごとに 7 **Your Honor**（身分の高い人に対する敬称で、ここは裁判長に向かっていっている） 9 **minute detail** 非常に細かい部分 11 **robot woman** 96ページに出てくるロボットのように動きのぎくしゃくした女性 13 **leafed through his file** 彼の書類をめくった 14 **fanning** うちわであおぎながら

16 **irrelevant** 無関係 17 **bearing** 意味、関係 21 **have her looked after and cared for**（だれかに）世話をしてもらったり、面倒をみてもらったりする 23 **didn't expect anything from each other** おたがいに対して何も期待していなかった 26 **dwell on** こだわる

without looking at me he stated that, with the court's permission, he would like to know whether I had gone back to the spring by myself intending to kill the Arab. "No," I said. Well, then, why was I armed and why did I return to precisely that spot? I said it just happened that way. And the prosecutor noted in a nasty voice, "That will be all for now." After that things got a little confused, at least for me. But after some conferring, the judge announced that the hearing was adjourned until the afternoon, at which time the witnesses would be heard.

I didn't even have time to think. I was taken out, put into the van, and driven to the prison, where I had something to eat. After a very short time, just long enough for me to realize I was tired, they came back for me; the whole thing started again, and I found myself in the same courtroom, in front of the same faces. Only it was much hotter, and as if by some miracle each member of the jury, the prosecutor, my lawyer, and some of the reporters, too, had been provided with straw fans. The young reporter and the little robot woman were still there. They weren't fanning themselves, but they were still watching me without saying a word.

I wiped away the sweat covering my face, and I had barely become aware of where I was and what I was doing when I heard the director of the home being called. He was asked whether Maman ever complained about me, and he said yes but that some of it was just a way the residents all had of complaining about their

1 **with the court's permission** 法廷の許可を得て 4 **armed** 武装した 5 **it just happened that way** たまたまそうなっただけだ 6 **noted** 指摘した **nasty** いやらしい 7 **That will be all for now** とりあえず、この件についてはここまでとします 8 **conferring** やりとり、打ち合わせ 9 **the hearing was adjourned until the afternoon** 午後まで閉廷とする 10 **witnesses would be heard** 証人が尋問される
29 **the residents** ホームの入居者

relatives. The judge had him clarify whether she used to reproach me for having put her in the home, and the director again said yes. But this time he didn't add anything else. To another question he replied that he had been surprised by my calm the day of the funeral. He was asked what he meant by "calm." The director then looked down at the tips of his shoes and said that I hadn't wanted to see Maman, that I hadn't cried once, and that I had left right after the funeral without paying my last respects at her grave. And one other thing had surprised him: one of the men who worked for the undertaker had told him I didn't know how old Maman was. There was a brief silence, and then the judge asked him if he was sure I was the man he had just been speaking of. The director didn't understand the question, so the judge told him, "It's a formality." He then asked the prosecutor if he had any questions to put to the witness, and the prosecutor exclaimed, "Oh no, that is quite sufficient!" with such glee and with such a triumphant look in my direction that for the first time in years I had this stupid urge to cry, because I could feel how much all these people hated me.

After asking the jury and my lawyer if they had any questions, the judge called the caretaker. The same ritual was repeated for him as for all the others. As he took the stand the caretaker glanced at me and then looked away. He answered the questions put to him. He said I hadn't wanted to see Maman, that I had smoked and slept some, and that I had had some coffee. It was then I

1 **clarify** 明確にする 2 **reproach** 非難する 5 **calm** 冷静さ 9 **right after the funeral** 葬儀の直後 **without paying my last respects at her grave** 母親の墓に最後のお別れをしないで 12 **undertaker** 葬儀屋 16 **formality** 形式、しきたり 18 **exclaimed** 大声でいった 19 **with such glee and with such a triumphant look in my direction** 喜びと勝ちほこった表情を私のほうに向けて

24 **ritual** 儀式 25 **he took the stand** 証人台に立った 29 **slept some** しばらく眠った

felt a stirring go through the room and for the first time I realized that I was guilty. The caretaker was asked to repeat the part about the coffee and the cigarette. The prosecutor looked at me with an ironic gleam in his eye. At that point my lawyer asked the caretaker if it wasn't true that he had smoked a cigarette with me. But the prosecutor objected vehemently to this question. "Who is on trial here and what kind of tactics are these, trying to taint the witnesses for the prosecution in an effort to detract from testimony that remains nonetheless overwhelming!" In spite of all that, the judge directed the caretaker to answer the question. The old man looked embarrassed and said, "I know I was wrong to do it. But I couldn't refuse the cigarette when monsieur offered it to me." Lastly, I was asked if I had anything to add. "Nothing," I said, "except that the witness is right. It's true, I did offer him a cigarette." The caretaker gave me a surprised and somehow grateful look. He hesitated and then he said that he was the one who offered me the coffee. My lawyer was exultant and stated loudly that the jury would take note of the fact. But the prosecutor shouted over our heads and said, "Indeed, the gentlemen of the jury will take note of the fact. And they will conclude that a stranger may offer a cup of coffee, but that beside the body of the one who brought him into the world, a son should have refused it." The caretaker went back to his bench.

When Thomas Pérez's turn came, a bailiff had to hold him up and help him get to the witness stand. Pérez said

1 **felt a stirring go through the room** 部屋の中がざわめくのを感じた　4 **ironic gleam** 皮肉な輝き　7 **objected** 反論した　**vehemently** 激しい調子で　8 **tactics** 戦術　9 **taint** 汚す、非難する　**the witnesses for the prosecution** 検察側の証人　10 **detract** そらす　**testimony** 証拠　**nonetheless** それにもかかわらず　**overwhelming** 決定的な　18 **grateful** 感謝に満ちた　20 **exultant** 大喜び　21 **take note** 注意を払う　25 **beside the body of the one** 遺骸のそばで　**brought him into the world** 自分をこの世に産みだしてくれた

it was really my mother he had known and that he had seen me only once, on the day of the funeral. He was asked how I had acted that day and he replied, "You understand, I was too sad. So I didn't see anything. My sadness made it impossible to see anything. Because for me it was a very great sadness. And I even fainted. So I wasn't able to see monsieur." The prosecutor asked him if he had at least seen me cry. Pérez answered no. The prosecutor in turn said, "The gentlemen of the jury will take note." But my lawyer got angry. He asked Pérez in what seemed to be an exaggerated tone of voice if he had seen me *not* cry. Pérez said, "No." The spectators laughed. And my lawyer, rolling up one of his sleeves, said with finality, "Here we have a perfect reflection of this entire trial: everything is true and nothing is true!" The prosecutor had a blank expression on his face, and with a pencil he was poking holes in the title page of his case file.

After a five-minute recess, during which my lawyer told me that everything was working out for the best, we heard the testimony of Céleste, who was called by the defense. "The defense" meant me. Every now and then Céleste would glance over in my direction and rotate his panama hat in his hands. He was wearing the new suit he used to put on to go with me to the races sometimes on Sundays. But I think he must not have been able to get his collar on, because he only had a brass stud keeping his shirt fastened. He was asked if I was a customer of his and he said, "Yes, but he was

9 **in turn** 今度は　13 **rolling up one of his sleeves** 袖をまくりながら　14 **with finality** きっぱりと　**perfect reflection of this entire trial** この裁判全体の完璧な反映　16 **blank expression** 無表情　17 **was poking holes** 穴を開けていた　**title page** 見出しのページ
19 **recess** 休憩　20 **working out for the best** うまくいっている　22 **The defense** 被告側　**"The defense" meant me**「被告」というのは私のことだ　24 **rotate** くるくる回す　**panama hat** パナマ帽（パナマソウの葉で編んだ日よけの帽子）　25 **races** 競馬　27 **get his collar on** カラーをつける　28 **brass stud** 真鍮のカラーボタン　**keeping his shirt fastened** シャツをとめる

also a friend"; what he thought of me, and he answered that I was a man; what he meant by that, and he stated that everybody knew what that meant; if he had noticed that I was ever withdrawn, and all he would admit was that I didn't speak unless I had something to say. The prosecutor asked him if I kept up with my bill. Céleste laughed and said, "Between us those were just details." He was again asked what he thought about my crime. He put his hands on the edge of the box, and you could tell he had something prepared. He said, "The way I see it, it's bad luck. Everybody knows what bad luck is. It leaves you defenseless. And there it is! The way I see it, it's bad luck." He was about to go on, but the judge told him that that would be all and thanked him. Céleste was a little taken aback. But he stated that he had more to say. He was asked to be brief. He again repeated that it was bad luck. And the judge said, "Yes, fine. But we are here to judge just this sort of bad luck. Thank you." And as if he had reached the end of both his knowledge and his goodwill, Céleste then turned toward me. It looked to me as if his eyes were glistening and his lips were trembling. He seemed to be asking me what else he could do. I said nothing; I made no gesture of any kind, but it was the first time in my life I ever wanted to kiss a man. The judge again instructed him to step down. Céleste went and sat among the spectators. He sat there throughout the entire trial, leaning forward, his elbows on his knees, the panama hat in his hands, listening to everything that was said.

1 **what he thought of me** 私のことをどう思っているか 2 **a man** 男らしい男 **that** = man 3 **if he had noticed that I was ever withdrawn** 私が内向的だということに気づいていたか 6 **kept up with my bill** つけをちゃんと払っていた 7 **Between us those were just details** われわれの間では、そんなのは取るに足りないことだ 9 **box** 証人台 **you could tell** (you は一般人称) だれでもわかるだろうが 10 **The way I see it** 自分がみるところによると 11 **It leaves you defenseless** It は bad luck。不運は人を無防備にしてしまう 12 **there it is!** まちがいない！ 15 **taken aback** 面食らった（まだ話すつもりでいたので） 16 **to be brief** 手短に 19 **had reached the end of both his knowledge and his goodwill** 知識も善意も尽きてしまった 25 **step down** 退がる 27 **throughout the entire trial** 公判が終わるまでずっと

Marie entered. She had put on a hat and she was still beautiful. But I liked her better with her hair loose. From where I was sitting, I could just make out the slight fullness of her breasts, and I recognized the little pout of her lower lip. She seemed very nervous. Right away she was asked how long she had known me. She said since the time she worked in our office. The judge wanted to know what her relation to me was. She said she was my friend. To another question she answered yes, it was true that she was supposed to marry me. Flipping through a file, the prosecutor asked her bluntly when our "liaison" had begun. She indicated the date. The prosecutor remarked indifferently that if he was not mistaken, that was the day after Maman died. Then in a slightly ironic tone he said that he didn't mean to dwell on such a delicate matter, and that he fully appreciated Marie's misgivings, but (and here his tone grew firmer) that he was duty bound to go beyond propriety. So he asked Marie to describe briefly that day when I had first known her. Marie didn't want to, but at the prosecutor's insistence, she went over our swim, the movies, and going back to my place. The prosecutor said that after Marie had given her statements to the examining magistrate, he had consulted the movie listings for that day. He added that Marie herself would tell the court what film was showing. In an almost expressionless voice she did in fact tell the court that it was a Fernandel film. By the time she had finished there was complete silence in the courtroom. The prosecutor then rose and,

2 **her hair loose** 髪を結んでいない 3 **make out** わかる 4 **fullness of her breasts** 胸の豊かさ 5 **pout** 突きだしている様子 11 **Flipping through** めくりながら **bluntly** ぶっきらぼうに 12 **liaison** 付き合い **indicated the date** 日にちをいった 15 **didn't mean to dwell on such a delicate matter** こういうデリケートなことにこだわるつもりはない 17 **misgivings** 懸念 18 **duty bound** 義務である **go beyond propriety** 失礼なことをする 21 **insistence** しつこさ **went over** 話した 23 **examining magistrate** 予審判事 24 **listings** タイトル 27 **Fernandel film** フェルナンデルの出ている映画

very gravely and with what struck me as real emotion in his voice, his finger pointing at me, said slowly and distinctly, "Gentlemen of the jury, the day after his mother's death, this man was out swimming, starting up a dubious liaison, and going to the movies, a comedy, for laughs. I have nothing further to say." He sat down in the still-silent courtroom. But all of a sudden Marie began to sob, saying it wasn't like that, there was more to it, and that she was being made to say the opposite of what she was thinking, that she knew me and I hadn't done anything wrong. But at a signal from the judge, the bailiff ushered her out and the trial proceeded.

Hardly anyone listened after that when Masson testified that I was an honest man "and I'd even say a decent one." Hardly anyone listened to Salamano either, when he recalled how I had been good to his dog and when he answered a question about my mother and me by saying that I had run out of things to say to Maman and that was why I'd put her in the home. "You must understand," Salamano kept saying, "you must understand." But no one seemed to understand. He was ushered out.

Next came Raymond, who was the last witness. He waved to me and all of a sudden, he blurted out that I was innocent. But the judge advised him that he was being asked not for judgments but for facts. He was instructed to wait for the questions before responding. He was directed to state precisely what his relations with the victim were. Raymond took this opportunity to say that he was the one the victim hated ever since he

5 **dubious** 不謹慎な　8 **sob** すすり泣く　**it wasn't like that** そんなんじゃない　9 **was being made to say the opposite of what she was thinking** 自分が思っているのと反対のことをいわされていた　11 **at a signal from the judge** 裁判長の合図で
12 **ushered** 証人席から退がらせた
14 **decent** 立派な　18 **run out of things to say** 話すことが尽きてしまった
23 **blurted out** 口走った　25 **not for judgments but for facts** 自分の判断（意見）ではなく、事実を　28 **victim** 被害者　**took this opportunity to say** この機会を捉えていった

had hit the guy's sister. Nevertheless, the judge asked him whether the victim hadn't also had reason to hate me. Raymond said that my being at the beach was just chance. The prosecutor then asked him how it was that the letter that set the whole drama in motion had been written by me. Raymond responded that it was just chance. The prosecutor retorted that chance already had a lot of misdeeds on its conscience in this case. He wanted to know if it was just by chance that I hadn't intervened when Raymond had beaten up his girlfriend, just by chance that I had acted as a witness at the police station, and again just by chance that my statements on that occasion had proved to be so convenient. Finishing up, he asked Raymond how he made his living, and when Raymond replied "warehouse guard," the prosecutor informed the jury that it was common knowledge that the witness practiced the profession of procurer. I was his friend and accomplice. They had before them the basest of crimes, a crime made worse than sordid by the fact that they were dealing with a monster, a man without morals. Raymond wanted to defend himself and my lawyer objected, but they were instructed that they must let the prosecutor finish. "I have little to add," the prosecutor said. "Was he your friend?" he asked Raymond. "Yes," Raymond said. "We were pals." The prosecutor then put the same question to me, and I looked at Raymond, who returned my gaze. I answered, "Yes." The prosecutor then turned to the jury and declared, "The same man who the day after his mother died was

3 **my being at the beach** 私が海岸にいたこと 4 **chance** 偶然 5 **set the whole drama in motion** このドラマ（事件）のきっかけとなった 7 **retorted** 言い返した 8 **misdeeds** 悪行、悪影響 **its conscience** 良心 10 **intervened** 止めに入る 13 **convenient** 便利な **Finishing up** 最後に 15 **warehouse guard** 倉庫番 16 **common knowledge** だれでも知っていること 17 **procurer** ポン引き（売春の斡旋をする男） 18 **accomplice** 共犯者 **They had before them** 検事やその他の人々が目前にしているのは 19 **the basest of crimes** 最低の犯罪 **sordid** いまわしい 20 **monster** 怪物のような人間 22 **were instructed** いわれた 25 **pals** 仲間 28 **declared** 断言した

indulging in the most shameful debauchery killed a man for the most trivial of reasons and did so in order to settle an affair of unspeakable vice."

He then sat down. But my lawyer had lost his patience, and, raising his hands so high that his sleeves fell, revealing the creases of a starched shirt, he shouted, "Come now, is my client on trial for burying his mother or for killing a man?" The spectators laughed. But the prosecutor rose to his feet again, adjusted his robe, and declared that only someone with the naiveté of his esteemed colleague could fail to appreciate that between these two sets of facts there existed a profound, fundamental, and tragic relationship. "Indeed," he loudly exclaimed, "I accuse this man of burying his mother with crime in his heart!" This pronouncement seemed to have a strong effect on the people in the courtroom. My lawyer shrugged his shoulders and wiped the sweat from his brow. But he looked shaken himself, and I realized that things weren't going well for me.

The trial was adjourned. As I was leaving the courthouse on my way back to the van, I recognized for a brief moment the smell and color of the summer evening. In the darkness of my mobile prison I could make out one by one, as if from the depths of my exhaustion, all the familiar sounds of a town I loved and of a certain time of day when I used to feel happy. The cries of the newspaper vendors in the already languid air, the last few birds in the square, the shouts of the sandwich sellers, the screech of the streetcars turning sharply through

1 **debauchery** 快楽　2 **trivial of reasons** 取るに足りない理由　3 **settle an affair of unspeakable vice** 口にするのもいまわしい悪行におよぶ
5 **his sleeves fell** 袖がずり下がった　6 **the creases of a starched shirt** 糊のきいたシャツの折り目　7 **Come now** ちょっと待って下さい　**client** 被告　9 **rose to his feet** 立ち上がった　10 **only someone with the naiveté of his esteemed colleague** 尊敬すべき同僚（弁護士のこと）のような無邪気さを持っている人間のみが　11 **could fail to appreciate that** that 以下のような真実を理解できない　12 **profound** 深刻な　17 **shrugged his shoulders** 肩をすくめた　18 **brow** 額　**looked shaken himself** 動揺しているようにみえた
20 **adjourned** 休廷になった　23 **mobile prison** 護送車　**make out** 聞き分ける　24 **exhaustion** 激しい疲労　27 **newspaper vendors** 新聞売り　**languid air** ものうい空気　28 **the square** 広場　29 **screech** きしる音

the upper town, and that hum in the sky before night engulfs the port: all this mapped out for me a route I knew so well before going to prison and which now I traveled blind. Yes, it was the hour when, a long time ago, I was perfectly content. What awaited me back then was always a night of easy, dreamless sleep. And yet something had changed, since it was back to my cell that I went to wait for the next day . . . as if familiar paths traced in summer skies could lead as easily to prison as to the sleep of the innocent.

1 **upper town** 高いところにある町　**hum** にぶい音、低い響き **engulfs** 飲みこむ　2 **mapped out for me a route** 道順を地図のように描いてくれた　3 **traveled blind** 外がみえない状況で走っている　5 **back then** 昔　6 **And yet** しかし　7 **since** なぜなら 8 **familiar paths** よく知っている道　9 **traced** 描かれた

4

Even in the prisoner's dock it's always interesting to hear people talk about you. And during the summations by the prosecutor and my lawyer, there was a lot said about me, maybe more about me than about my crime. But were their two speeches so different after all? My lawyer raised his arms and pleaded guilty, but with an explanation. The prosecutor waved his hands and proclaimed my guilt, but without an explanation. One thing bothered me a little, though. Despite everything that was on my mind, I felt like intervening every now and then, but my lawyer kept telling me, "Just keep quiet—it won't do your case any good." In a way, they seemed to be arguing the case as if it had nothing to do with me. Everything was happening without my participation. My fate was being decided without anyone so much as asking my opinion. There were times when I felt like breaking in on all of them and saying, "Wait a minute! Who's the accused here? Being the accused counts for something. And I have something to say!" But on second thought, I didn't have anything to say. Besides, I have to admit that whatever interest you can get people to take in you doesn't last very long. For example, I got bored very quickly with the prosecutor's speech. Only bits and pieces—a gesture or a long but isolated tirade—caught my attention or aroused my interest.

The gist of what he was saying, if I understood him correctly, was that my crime was premeditated. At least

3 **prisoner's dock** 被告席　4 **summations** 最終弁論　7 **two speeches** 弁護士と検事の弁論　8 **pleaded guilty** 有罪を認めた　**with an explanation** 釈明がついている　11 **Despite everything that was on my mind** いろんなことを心に留めていたものの　12 **intervening** 口をはさむ　14 **do your case any good** あなたの件が有利になる　17 **so much as** ～も　19 **breaking in on all of them** 弁論をしている連中に割って入って　20 **the accused** 被告人　**counts for something** 大きな意味を持っている　21 **on second thought** よく考えてみると　23 **get people to take in you** 人に自分のことで興味を持ってもらう　24 **doesn't last very long**（主語は whatever ～ in you まで）あまり長続きしない　26 **bits and pieces** 細切れの断片　**isolated tirade** 前後の文脈のない長広舌
28 **gist** 要点　29 **premeditated** 前もって計画していた

that is what he tried to show. As he himself said, "I will prove it to you, gentlemen, and I will prove it in two ways. First, in the blinding clarity of the facts, and second, in the dim light cast by the mind of this criminal soul." He reminded the court of my insensitivity; of my ignorance when asked Maman's age; of my swim the next day—with a woman; of the Fernandel movie; and finally of my taking Marie home with me. It took me a few minutes to understand the last part because he kept saying "his mistress" and to me she was Marie. Then he came to the business with Raymond. I thought his way of viewing the events had a certain consistency. What he was saying was plausible. I had agreed with Raymond to write the letter in order to lure his mistress and submit her to mistreatment by a man "of doubtful morality." I had provoked Raymond's adversaries at the beach. Raymond had been wounded. I had asked him to give me his gun. I had gone back alone intending to use it. I had shot the Arab as I planned. I had waited. And to make sure I had done the job right, I fired four more shots, calmly, point-blank—thoughtfully, as it were.

"And there you have it, gentlemen," said the prosecutor. "I have retraced for you the course of events which led this man to kill with full knowledge of his actions. I stress this point," he said, "for this is no ordinary murder, no thoughtless act for which you might find mitigating circumstances. This man, gentlemen, this man is intelligent. You heard him, didn't you? He knows how to answer. He knows the value of words. And no one can

3 **blinding clarity of the facts** 明々白々たる事実　5 **reminded the court of my insensitivity** 法廷の人々に私の無神経さ、冷酷さを思い出させた　10 **his mistress** 彼の女　**to me she was Marie**（検事は「女」と呼んだが、）私にとってはマリーだ　11 **the business with Raymond** レイモンの起こした事件　12 **consistency** 一貫性　13 **plausible** ありえそうな　14 **lure** おびき寄せる　15 **submit** ～を受けさせる　**mistreatment** 虐待　**doubtful morality** 道徳心の疑わしい　16 **provoked** 挑発した　**adversaries** 敵　21 **point-blank** ねらいを定めて　**thoughtfully** 考えたうえで　**as it were** いってみれば

22 **there you have it** 以上です　23 **retraced** なぞってみた　24 **with full knowledge of his actions** 自分の行動を十分に理解している　26 **mitigating circumstances** 酌量の余地のある事件　27 **intelligent** 理性がある、理性的に考えることができる

say that he acted without realizing what he was doing."

I was listening, and I could hear that I was being judged intelligent. But I couldn't quite understand how an ordinary man's good qualities could become crushing accusations against a guilty man. At least that was what struck me, and I stopped listening to the prosecutor until I heard him say, "Has he so much as expressed any remorse? Never, gentlemen. Not once during the preliminary hearings did this man show emotion over his heinous offense." At that point, he turned in my direction, pointed his finger at me, and went on attacking me without my ever really understanding why. Of course, I couldn't help admitting that he was right. I didn't feel much remorse for what I'd done. But I was surprised by how relentless he was. I would have liked to have tried explaining to him cordially, almost affectionately, that I had never been able to truly feel remorse for anything. My mind was always on what was coming next, today or tomorrow. But naturally, given the position I'd been put in, I couldn't talk to anyone in that way. I didn't have the right to show any feeling or goodwill. And I tried to listen again, because the prosecutor started talking about my soul.

He said that he had peered into it and that he had found nothing, gentlemen of the jury. He said the truth was that I didn't have a soul and that nothing human, not one of the moral principles that govern men's hearts, was within my reach. "Of course," he added, "we cannot blame him for this. We cannot complain that he lacks

4 **good qualities** 長所　**crushing accusations** すさまじい非難 6 **struck** 驚かせた　7 **so much as** ～さえ　8 **remorse** 後悔、悔恨　**preliminary hearings** 予審　10 **heinous offense** 憎むべき、凶悪な犯罪　12 **without my ever really understanding why** 私の本当の理解なしに（私にはちっとも理解できなかった） 15 **relentless** 無慈悲な　18 **My mind was always on what was coming next** 私の頭は常に、これから先のことを考えていた 19 **given the position I'd been put in**（givenは仮定を表わす）もし私がこのような状況に置かれたら

24 **peered into it** それ（私の魂）をのぞいてみた　27 **moral principles** 道徳的な理念　**govern men's heart** 人間の心を支配する　28 **within my reach** 手の届く範囲内にある

what it was not in his power to acquire. But here in this court the wholly negative virtue of tolerance must give way to the sterner but loftier virtue of justice. Especially when the emptiness of a man's heart becomes, as we find it has in this man, an abyss threatening to swallow up society." It was then that he talked about my attitude toward Maman. He repeated what he had said earlier in the proceedings. But it went on much longer than when he was talking about my crime—so long, in fact, that finally all I was aware of was how hot a morning it was. At least until the prosecutor stopped and after a short silence continued in a very low voice filled with conviction: "Tomorrow, gentlemen, this same court is to sit in judgment of the most monstrous of crimes: the murder of a father." According to him, the imagination recoiled before such an odious offense. He went so far as to hope that human justice would mete out punishment unflinchingly. But he wasn't afraid to say it: my callousness inspired in him a horror nearly greater than that which he felt at the crime of parricide. And also according to him, a man who is morally guilty of killing his mother severs himself from society in the same way as the man who raises a murderous hand against the father who begat him. In any case, the one man paved the way for the deeds of the other, in a sense foreshadowed and even legitimized them. "I am convinced, gentlemen," he added, raising his voice, "that you will not think it too bold of me if I suggest to you that the man who is seated in the dock is also guilty of the murder to be tried in this court

1 **what it was not in his power to acquire** 彼の力では獲得できないもの　2 **wholly negative virtue of tolerance must give way to the sterner but loftier virtue of justice** 寛容というまったく消極的な美徳は、正義という厳しいが崇高な美徳に場所を譲らなくてはならない　4 **becomes**（an abyss に続く。as we find it has in this man は挿入句）　5 **it** = the emptiness of a man's heart **abyss** 底無しの淵　6 **It was then that**（It was...that の強調構文）　12 **filled with conviction** 確信に満ちて　13 **this same court** まさにこの法廷が　**sit in judgment** 裁判を行う　14 **the most monstrous of crimes** 最もおそろしい犯罪　15 **recoiled** たじろぐ　16 **odious offense** 忌まわしい罪　**went so far as** 〜までもした　17 **mete out** 与える　**unflinchingly** たじろぐことなく　18 **callousness** 無感覚　20 **parricide** 親殺し　21 **morally guilty of killing his mother** 道徳的にみての母親殺し　22 **severs** 切り離す　23 **begat** この世に産んだ　24 **paved the way** 道を開いた　**for the deeds of the other** もうひとりの人間の行為のため　25 **foreshadowed** 前兆となった　**legitimized** 正しいとする　27 **it**（次の行の if 以下のこと）　29 **to be tried** 裁かれる

tomorrow. He must be punished accordingly." Here the prosecutor wiped his face, which was glistening with sweat. He concluded by saying that his duty was a painful one but that he would carry it out resolutely. He stated that I had no place in a society whose most fundamental rules I ignored and that I could not appeal to the same human heart whose elementary response I knew nothing of. "I ask you for this man's head," he said, "and I do so with a heart at ease. For if in the course of what has been a long career I have had occasion to call for the death penalty, never as strongly as today have I felt this painful duty made easier, lighter, clearer by the certain knowledge of a sacred imperative and by the horror I feel when I look into a man's face and all I see is a monster."

When the prosecutor returned to his seat, there was a rather long silence. My head was spinning with heat and astonishment. The presiding judge cleared his throat and in a very low voice asked me if I had anything to add. I stood up, and since I did wish to speak, I said, almost at random, in fact, that I never intended to kill the Arab. The judge replied by saying that at least that was an assertion, that until then he hadn't quite grasped the nature of my defense, and that before hearing from my lawyer he would be happy to have me state precisely the motives for my act. Fumbling a little with my words and realizing how ridiculous I sounded, I blurted out that it was because of the sun. People laughed. My lawyer threw up his hands, and immediately after that he was

1 **accordingly** 相応に、しかるべく　4 **carry it out** やりとげる **resolutely** 断固として、決然と　5 **whose fundamental rule** (whose の先行詞は a society) その基本的なルール　7 **whose elementary response** (先行詞は the same human heart) その根本的な反応　8 **ask you for this man's head** この男の死刑を要求する　9 **heart at ease** 心はおだやかだ　**For** なぜなら　**in the course of what has been a long career** 長年検事を務めてきたが、そのなかで　10 **I have had occasion to call for the death penalty** 死刑を求刑する機会があった　11 **never as strongly as today have I felt this painful duty made easier, lighter, clearer** 今日ほど強く、このつらい義務を、容易で、軽くて、明確に感じたことがない　12 **by the certain knowledge of a sacred imperative** 神聖な強制力の確かな認識（宗教的にみて、まちがいないという確信）によって　14 **when I look into a man's face and all I see is a monster** 人の顔をみて、そこにみえるのが怪物であるとき

17 **spinning** くらくらしていた　18 **cleared his throat** 咳払いをした　21 **at random** でたらめに　22 **replied by saying that at least that was an assertion** 少なくともそれはひとつの主張であると答えた　23 **grasped**　把握した、理解した　**the nature of my defense** 私の主張（弁護）の本質　26 **Fumbling a little with my words** 少し言葉に詰まりながら　27 **how ridiculous I sounded** 自分のいうことがどんなにばかげてきこえるか **blurted out** 口走った　28 **it was because of the sun** 太陽（陽射し）のせいだった

given the floor. But he stated that it was late and that he would need several hours. He requested that the trial be reconvened in the afternoon. The court granted his motion.

That afternoon the big fans were still churning the thick air in the courtroom and the jurors' brightly colored fans were all moving in unison. It seemed to me as if my lawyer's summation would never end. At one point, though, I listened, because he was saying, "It is true I killed a man." He went on like that, saying "I" whenever he was speaking about me. I was completely taken aback. I leaned over to one of the guards and asked him why he was doing that. He told me to keep quiet, and a few seconds later he added, "All lawyers do it." I thought it was a way to exclude me even further from the case, reduce me to nothing, and, in a sense, substitute himself for me. But I think I was already very far removed from that courtroom. Besides, my lawyer seemed ridiculous to me. He rushed through a plea of provocation, and then he too talked about my soul. But to me he seemed to be a lot less talented than the prosecutor. "I, too," he said, "have peered into this man's soul, but unlike the esteemed representative of the government prosecutor's office, I did see something there, and I can assure you that I read it like an open book." What he read was that I was an honest man, a steadily employed, tireless worker, loyal to the firm that employed him, well liked, and sympathetic to the misfortunes of others. To him, I was a model son who

1 **given the floor** 発言を許された 2 **be reconvened** 再開される 3 **granted his motion**（法廷は）彼の提案を受け入れた 5 **churning** かきまわす 6 **jurors'** 陪審員たちの 7 **in unison** 同じように 12 **taken aback** 驚いた **leaned over** 体を傾けた 14 **All lawyers do it** 弁護士はみんなああいうふうにする 15 **exclude** 除外する 16 **reduce me to nothing** 私を無にしてしまう 17 **substitute himself for me** 彼を私の代わりにする 18 **removed** 遠ざけられている 19 **rushed through** 大急ぎで終わらせた **a plea of provocation** 犯罪の弁護 23 **esteemed representative** 尊敬すべき代表者 24 **the government prosecutor's office** 政府の検察局 27 **steadily employed** ちゃんと働いている **tireless worker** 勤勉な労働者 **firm** 会社 28 **well liked**（みんなに）とても好かれている

had supported his mother as long as he could. In the end I had hoped that a home for the aged would give the old woman the comfort that with my limited means I could not provide for her. "Gentlemen," he added, "I am amazed that so much has been made of this home. For after all, if it were necessary to prove the usefulness and importance of such institutions, all one would have to say is that it is the state itself which subsidizes them." The only thing is, he didn't say anything about the funeral, and I thought that that was a glaring omission in his summation. But all the long speeches, all the interminable days and hours that people had spent talking about my soul, had left me with the impression of a colorless swirling river that was making me dizzy.

In the end, all I remember is that while my lawyer went on talking, I could hear through the expanse of chambers and courtrooms an ice cream vendor blowing his tin trumpet out in the street. I was assailed by memories of a life that wasn't mine anymore, but one in which I'd found the simplest and most lasting joys: the smells of summer, the part of town I loved, a certain evening sky, Marie's dresses and the way she laughed. The utter pointlessness of whatever I was doing there seized me by the throat, and all I wanted was to get it over with and get back to my cell and sleep. I barely even heard when my lawyer, wrapping up, exclaimed that the jury surely would not send an honest, hardworking man to his death because he had lost control of himself for one moment, and then he asked them to find

2 **the aged** 老人たち 3 **limited means** 限られた収入 5 **so much has been made of this home** このホームのことがあれほど大きく取り立てられた 7 **such institutions** あのような施設 8 **state itself** 国自体 **subsidizes** 助成金を出している 10 **glaring omission** 紛れもない手抜かり 11 **summation** 最終弁論 12 **interminable days and hours** 延々と続く日々、時間 14 **swirling river** 渦巻く川 **dizzy** めまいのする

16 **the expanse of chambers and courtrooms** いくつもの部屋や法廷のむこうから 17 **an ice cream vendor** アイスクリーム売り 18 **tin trumpet** ブリキのラッパ **was assailed** 襲われた 19 **one** = memory 20 **most lasting joys** とても長続きのする喜び 23 **utter pointlessness** まったくの無意味 24 **seized me by the throat** 私の喉をつかんだ **get it over with** 終わりにする 26 **wrapping up** 仕上げに 28 **he had lost control of himself** 彼が自制心をなくしていた

extenuating circumstances for a crime for which I was already suffering the most agonizing of punishments—eternal remorse. Court was adjourned and my lawyer sat back down. He looked exhausted. But his colleagues came over to shake his hand. I heard: "That was brilliant!" One of them even appealed to me as a witness. "Wasn't it?" he said. I agreed, but my congratulations weren't sincere, because I was too tired.

Meanwhile, the sun was getting low outside and it wasn't as hot anymore. From what street noises I could hear, I sensed the sweetness of evening coming on. There we all were, waiting. And what we were all waiting for really concerned only me. I looked around the room again. Everything was the same as it had been the first day. My eyes met those of the little robot woman and the reporter in the gray jacket. That reminded me that I hadn't tried to catch Marie's eye once during the whole trial. I hadn't forgotten about her; I'd just had too much to do. I saw her sitting between Céleste and Raymond. She made a little gesture as if to say "At last." There was a worried little smile on her face. But my heart felt nothing, and I couldn't even return her smile.

The judges came back in. Very quickly a series of questions was read to the jury. I heard "guilty of murder" . . . "premeditated" . . . "extenuating circumstances." The jurors filed out, and I was taken to the little room where I had waited before. My lawyer joined me. He was very talkative and spoke to me more confidently and cordially than he ever had before. He thought that

1 **extenuating** 酌量すべき 2 **agonizing** 苦痛 3 **eternal remorse** 永遠の悔恨 4 **sat back down** 椅子に座った 6 **appealed to me as a witness** 私にも証人になるよう訴えた
7 **Wasn't it?** そうだったでしょう？ **congratulations** 称賛
12 **There we all were, waiting** 私たちは全員、そこで待っていた **what we were all waiting for really concerned only me** 私たち全員が待っていたことは、実際は、私にしか関係のないことだった 20 **At last** やっと、ようやく
25 **premeditated** 前もって計画していた **extenuating circumstances** 酌量すべき状況 26 **filed out** 並んで出ていった
28 **talkative** 口数が多い **confidently** 自信たっぷりに

everything would go well and that I would get off with a few years in prison or at hard labor. I asked him whether he thought there was any chance of overturning the verdict if it was unfavorable. He said no. His tactic had been not to file any motions so as not to antagonize the jury. He explained to me that verdicts weren't set aside just like that, for nothing. That seemed obvious and I accepted his logic. Looking at it objectively, it made perfect sense. Otherwise there would be too much pointless paperwork. "Anyway," he said, "we can always appeal. But I'm convinced that the outcome will be favorable."

We waited a long time—almost three-quarters of an hour, I think. Then a bell rang. My lawyer left me, saying, "The foreman of the jury is going to announce the verdict. You'll only be brought in for the passing of sentence." Doors slammed. People were running on stairs somewhere, but I couldn't tell if they were nearby or far away. Then I heard a muffled voice reading something in the courtroom. When the bell rang again, when the door to the dock opened, what rose to meet me was the silence in the courtroom, silence and the strange feeling I had when I noticed that the young reporter had turned his eyes away. I didn't look in Marie's direction. I didn't have time to, because the presiding judge told me in bizarre language that I was to have my head cut off in a public square in the name of the French people. Then it seemed to me that I suddenly knew what was on everybody's face. It was a look of consideration, I'm sure. The policemen were very gentle with me. The

2 **at hard labor** 重労働についていた 3 **overturning** ひっくり返す 4 **verdict** 判決 **unfavorable** 好ましくない **tactic** 作戦 5 **file any motions** （刑の軽重について）提案する **so as not to antagonize** 印象を悪くしないように 6 **verdicts weren't set aside** 判決は無効にならない 7 **for nothing** 理由もないのに 8 **objectively** 客観的に **it made perfect sense** まったく筋が通っている 9 **pointless paperwork** 意味もない書類仕事 10 **appeal** 上訴
14 **foreman** 代表 15 **for the passing of sentence** 判決の言い渡し 16 **slammed** 大きな音を立てて閉まった 18 **muffled voice** ぼんやりきこえる声 23 **turned his eyes away** 目をそらした 25 **bizarre** 奇妙な、奇怪な 26 **public square** 公共の広場 **in the name of the French people** フランス国民の名において 28 **a look of consideration** 思いやりの表情

lawyer put his hand on my wrist. I wasn't thinking about anything anymore. But the presiding judge asked me if I had anything to say. I thought about it. I said, "No." That's when they took me away.

5

For the third time I've refused to see the chaplain. I don't have anything to say to him; I don't feel like talking, and I'll be seeing him soon enough as it is. All I care about right now is escaping the machinery of justice, seeing if there's any way out of the inevitable. They've put me in a different cell. From this one, when I'm stretched out on my bunk, I see the sky and that's all I see. I spend my days watching how the dwindling of color turns day into night. Lying here, I put my hands behind my head and wait. I can't count the times I've wondered if there have ever been any instances of condemned men escaping the relentless machinery, disappearing before the execution or breaking through the cordon of police. Then I blame myself every time for not having paid enough attention to accounts of executions. A man should always take an interest in those things. You never know what might happen. I'd read stories in the papers like everybody else. But there must have been books devoted to the subject that I'd never been curious enough to look into. Maybe I would have found some accounts of escapes in them. I might have discovered that in at least one instance the wheel had stopped, that in spite of all the unrelenting calculation, chance and luck had, at least once, changed something. Just once! In a way, I think that would have been enough. My heart would have taken over from there. The papers were always talking about the debt owed to

3 **For the third time** 3度　**chaplain** 司祭　5 **as it is** 実際は 6 **machinery of justice** 裁判の仕組み　7 **any way out of the inevitable** 逃れられないことからの逃げ道　8 **one** = cell　9 **stretched out** 体を伸ばした　**bunk** 作り付けのベッド 10 **dwindling of color** 色が薄れていくこと　13 **condemned** 死刑を宣告された　14 **relentless machinery** 無慈悲な道具 15 **execution** 処刑　**breaking through** 突破する　16 **cordon** 非常線　17 **accounts** 話、例　21 **devoted to the subject** そのことを詳しく書いた　23 **accounts of escapes** 逃亡に関する話、例　24 **one instance the wheel had stopped** その車輪（運命の輪）が止まったひとつの例　25 **unrelenting calculation** 無慈悲な（非人間的な）前もっての計画　26 **chance** 偶然 27 **that would have been enough** それで（たった1度で）十分だろう　28 **would have taken over from there** そこから先を引き継ぐだろう　29 **The papers** 新聞　**the debt owed to society** 社会に対する責任

society. According to them, it had to be paid. But that doesn't speak to the imagination. What really counted was the possibility of escape, a leap to freedom, out of the implacable ritual, a wild run for it that would give whatever chance for hope there was. Of course, hope meant being cut down on some street corner, as you ran like mad, by a random bullet. But when I really thought it through, nothing was going to allow me such a luxury. Everything was against it; I would just be caught up in the machinery again.

Despite my willingness to understand, I just couldn't accept such arrogant certainty. Because, after all, there really was something ridiculously out of proportion between the verdict such certainty was based on and the imperturbable march of events from the moment the verdict was announced. The fact that the sentence had been read at eight o'clock at night and not at five o'clock, the fact that it could have been an entirely different one, the fact that it had been decided by men who change their underwear, the fact that it had been handed down in the name of some vague notion called the French (or German, or Chinese) people—all of it seemed to detract from the seriousness of the decision. I was forced to admit, however, that from the moment it had been passed its consequences became as real and as serious as the wall against which I pressed the length of my body.

At times like this I remembered a story Maman used to tell me about my father. I never knew him. Maybe the only thing I did know about the man was the story

2 **speak to** 語りかける、訴える **What really counted** 本当に重要なこと 3 **out of the implacable ritual** 無慈悲な儀式を逃れて 4 **a wild run for it** それ（逃亡）にむかっての必死の疾走 5 **hope meant** 希望は意味する 6 **being cut down** 殺される（by a random bullet「流れ弾に当たって」） 8 **through** 十分に **such a luxury** そんな贅沢 9 **against** 逆らっている、邪魔をしている **it** = such a luxury **caught up** つかまる

12 **arrogant certainty** 傲慢な確実性（逃れることのできない死） **there really was something ridiculously out of proportion** ばかばかしいほどアンバランスな何かがあった（between ① and ②「①と②の間に」） 14 ① **the verdict such certainty was based on** そのような確実性の基盤となっている判決 ② **the imperturbable march of events** 動かすことのできない一連の出来事 16 **sentence** 判決 19 **change their underwear** 下着を着替える 21 **notion** 概念 22 **detract from** ～をそこなう 23 **was forced to** ～せざるをえなかった 24 **it** = sentence 25 **as real and as serious as the wall** この壁と同じくらい現実的で厳然としている 26 **pressed the length of my body** 私が全身を押しつけている

27 **At times like this** こんなときには

Maman would tell me back then: he'd gone to watch a murderer be executed. Just the thought of going had made him sick to his stomach. But he went anyway, and when he came back he spent half the morning throwing up. I remember feeling a little disgusted by him at the time. But now I understood, it was perfectly normal. How had I not seen that there was nothing more important than an execution, and that when you come right down to it, it was the only thing a man could truly be interested in? If I ever got out of this prison I would go and watch every execution there was. But I think it was a mistake even to consider the possibility. Because at the thought that one fine morning I would find myself a free man standing behind a cordon of police—on the outside, as it were—at the thought of being the spectator who comes to watch and then can go and throw up afterwards, a wave of poisoned joy rose in my throat. But I wasn't being reasonable. It was a mistake to let myself get carried away by such imaginings, because the next minute I would get so cold that I would curl up into a ball under my blanket and my teeth would be chattering and I couldn't make them stop.

But naturally, you can't always be reasonable. At other times, for instance, I would make up new laws. I would reform the penal code. I'd realized that the most important thing was to give the condemned man a chance. Even one in a thousand was good enough to set things right. So it seemed to me that you could come up with a mixture of chemicals that if ingested by the

1 **back then** 昔 2 **be executed** 処刑された 4 **half the morning** 午前中の半分 **throwing up** 吐く 8 **you come right down to it** つまるところ、結局 12 **consider the possibility** その可能性を考える **Because...a wave of poisoned joy rose in my throat** なぜなら（①や②を考えると）苦い喜びの波が喉までせり上がってくるからだ ① **at the thought that one fine morning I would find myself a free man standing behind a cordon of police** ある晴れた朝、自分が警察の非常線のむこうで自由になっていると考えると 15 ② **at the thought of being the spectator who** who以下のような見物人になっていると考えると 18 **I wasn't being reasonable** 私はばかばかしいことを考えていた 20 **curl up into a ball** 体をボールのように丸める
21 **chattering** かちかち鳴る
23 **you**（一般人称） 25 **penal code** 刑法典 26 **condemned man** 死刑を宣告された人間 27 **Even one in a thousand was good enough to set things right** 千にひとつのチャンスで、ことを正すには十分だ 28 **come up with a mixture of chemicals** 化学薬品を考えつく 29 **ingested by the patient** 患者によって摂取される

patient (that's the word I'd use: "patient") would kill him nine times out of ten. But he would know this—that would be the one condition. For by giving it some hard thought, by considering the whole thing calmly, I could see that the trouble with the guillotine was that you had no chance at all, absolutely none. The fact was that it had been decided once and for all that the patient was to die. It was an open-and-shut case, a fixed arrangement, a tacit agreement that there was no question of going back on. If by some extraordinary chance the blade failed, they would just start over. So the thing that bothered me most was that the condemned man had to hope the machine would work the first time. And I say that's wrong. And in a way I was right. But in another way I was forced to admit that that was the whole secret of good organization. In other words, the condemned man was forced into a kind of moral collaboration. It was in his interest that everything go off without a hitch.

I was also made to see that until that moment I'd had mistaken ideas about these things. For a long time I believed—and I don't know why—that to get to the guillotine you had to climb stairs onto a scaffold. I think it was because of the French Revolution—I mean, because of everything I'd been taught or shown about it. But one morning I remembered seeing a photograph that appeared in the papers at the time of a much-talked-about execution. In reality, the machine was set up right on the ground, as simple as you please. It was much narrower than I'd thought. It was funny I'd never noticed that

1 **that's the word I'd use: "Patient"** 私は（死刑囚という言葉ではなく）患者という言葉を使いたい 2 **that would be the one condition** それがひとつの条件になる 3 **giving it some hard thought** それを現実的に考えること 5 **guillotine** ギロチン、斬首台 7 **once and for all** それっきり 8 **open-and-shut case** 単純明快な事実 **fixed arrangement** 変えようのないやり方 9 **tacit agreement** 暗黙の了解 **going back on** 取り消す 10 **the blade** ギロチンの刃 11 **just start over** やり直すだけ 15 **whole secret of good organization** よき組織の秘密 17 **moral collaboration** 精神的協力 **It**（that 以下のこと） **was in his interest** 彼のためになる 18 **everything go off** すべてがうまくいく **without a hitch** 滞りなく

22 **scaffold** 処刑台 26 **much-talked-about execution** しきりに話題になっていた処刑 28 **as simple as you please** まったく単純な

before. I'd been struck by this picture because the guillotine looked like such a precision instrument, perfect and gleaming. You always get exaggerated notions of things you don't know anything about. I was made to see that contrary to what I thought, everything was very simple: the guillotine is on the same level as the man approaching it. He walks up to it the way you walk up to another person. That bothered me too. Mounting the scaffold, going right up into the sky, was something the imagination could hold on to. Whereas, once again, the machine destroyed everything: you were killed discreetly, with a little shame and with great precision.

There were two other things I was always thinking about: the dawn and my appeal. I would reason with myself, though, and try not to think about them anymore. I would stretch out, look at the sky, and force myself to find something interesting about it. It would turn green: that was evening. I would make another effort to divert my thoughts. I would listen to my heartbeat. I couldn't imagine that this sound which had been with me for so long could ever stop. I've never really had much of an imagination. But still I would try to picture the exact moment when the beating of my heart would no longer be going on inside my head. But it was no use. The dawn or my appeal would still be there. I would end up telling myself that the most rational thing was not to hold myself back.

They always came at dawn, I knew that. And so I spent my nights waiting for that dawn. I've never liked

2 **precision instrument** 精密な道具　3 **gleaming** 輝いている　**You always get exaggerated notions of things you don't know anything about**（You は一般人称）人はいつも、自分の知らないものについては誇張した考えを持つものだ（大げさに考えるものだ）　6 **level** 高さ　7 **the way you walk up to another person** ほかの人のほうに歩いていくのと同じように　10 **hold on to** しがみつく　11 **discreetly** 慎重に　12 **great precision** じつに正確に

14 **the dawn and my appeal** 夜明けと上訴　**reason with myself** 自分にいいきかせる　16 **stretch out**（ベッドに）体を伸ばす　19 **divert my thought** 考えをそらす、ほかのことを考える　20 **which had been with me for so long** これまで長く自分といっしょだった　24 **it was no use** むだだった　26 **end up telling myself** 結局、自分にこういう　**the most rational thing was not to hold myself back** 最も賢いのは、自分を抑えようとしないことだ

being surprised. If something is going to happen to me, I want to be there. That's why I ended up sleeping only a little bit during the day and then, all night long, waited patiently for the first light to show on the pane of sky. The hardest time was that uncertain hour when I knew they usually set to work. After midnight, I would wait and watch. My ears had never heard so many noises or picked up such small sounds. One thing I can say, though, is that in a certain way I was lucky that whole time, since I never heard footsteps. Maman used to say that you can always find something to be happy about. In my prison, when the sky turned red and a new day slipped into my cell, I found out that she was right. Because I might just as easily have heard footsteps and my heart could have burst. Even though I would rush to the door at the slightest shuffle, even though, with my ear pressed to the wood, I would wait frantically until I heard the sound of my own breathing, terrified to find it so hoarse, like a dog's panting, my heart would not burst after all, and I would have gained another twenty-four hours.

All day long there was the thought of my appeal. I think I got everything out of it that I could. I would assess my holdings and get the maximum return on my thoughts. I would always begin by assuming the worst: my appeal was denied. "Well, so I'm going to die." Sooner than other people will, obviously. But everybody knows life isn't worth living. Deep down I knew perfectly well that it doesn't much matter whether you

3 **during the day** 昼間　4 **patiently** 我慢強く　**the pane of sky** 天窓　5 **The hardest time** 最もつらい時間　**uncertain hour** 不安定な時間　6 **they usually set to work** 彼らがいつも仕事にとりかかる　9 **that whole time** そのときはずっと　12 **a new day slipped into my cell** 新しい日がこっそり私の独房に忍びこんだ　16 **the slightest shuffle** かすかな足音　17 **frantically** 必死に　19 **it** = the sound of my own breathing　**hoarse** 荒い　**panting** あえぎ

23 **got everything out of it** (it = the thought of my appeal) それからすべてを得た　**that I could** できる限りの　**assess my holdings** 自分の持っているものを算定する　24 **the maximum return** 最大限の見返り　25 **assuming the worst** 最悪の事態を仮定する　27 **Sooner than other people will** ほかの人より先に　28 **Deep down** 心の底では

die at thirty or at seventy, since in either case other men and women will naturally go on living—and for thousands of years. In fact, nothing could be clearer. Whether it was now or twenty years from now, I would still be the one dying. At that point, what would disturb my train of thought was the terrifying leap I would feel my heart take at the idea of having twenty more years of life ahead of me. But I simply had to stifle it by imagining what I'd be thinking in twenty years when it would all come down to the same thing anyway. Since we're all going to die, it's obvious that when and how don't matter. Therefore (and the difficult thing was not to lose sight of all the reasoning that went into this "therefore"), I had to accept the rejection of my appeal.

Then and only then would I have the right, so to speak—would I give myself permission, as it were—to consider the alternative hypothesis: I was pardoned. The trouble was that I would somehow have to cool the hot blood that would suddenly surge through my body and sting my eyes with a delirious joy. It would take all my strength to quiet my heart, to be rational. In order to make my resignation to the first hypothesis more plausible, I had to be level-headed about this one as well. If I succeeded, I gained an hour of calm. That was something anyway.

It was at one such moment that I once again refused to see the chaplain. I was lying down, and I could tell from the golden glow in the sky that evening was coming on. I had just denied my appeal and I could feel the

3 **nothing could be clearer** これほどはっきりしていることはない　4 **I would still be the one dying** 私は死ぬべき存在なのだ　6 **my train of thought** 思考の流れ　**the terrifying leap I would feel my heart take** 私が感じる心臓が飛び上がるくらいの恐ろしい動揺　7 **at the idea of having twenty more years of life ahead of me** これから先20年生きると思うと　8 **stifle** 圧し殺す　9 **in twenty years** 20年後　**it would all come down to the same thing** 結局おなじことになる　11 **when and how don't matter** いつ死ぬか、どうして死ぬかは問題ではない（どうでもいい）　12 **Therefore** したがって　**to lose sight of all the reasoning that went into this "therefore"** この「したがって」に収斂する（帰結する）論理を見失う　14 **rejection of my appeal** 上訴が認められないこと
15 **Then and only then** そうすれば、そして、そうしたときにだけ　17 **hypothesis** 仮定　18 **somehow** なんとかして　19 **surge through my body** この体を激しく揺さぶる　20 **sting** 刺激する　**delirious** 狂おしいほどの　22 **resignation** 断念　**plausible** 受け入れやすい　23 **level-headed** 冷静　24 **That was something** それはそれなりに素晴らしいことだった
27 **chaplain** 司祭

steady pulse of my blood circulating inside me. I didn't need to see the chaplain. For the first time in a long time I thought about Marie. The days had been long since she'd stopped writing. That evening I thought about it and told myself that maybe she had gotten tired of being the girlfriend of a condemned man. It also occurred to me that maybe she was sick, or dead. These things happen. How was I to know, since apart from our two bodies, now separated, there wasn't anything to keep us together or even to remind us of each other? Anyway, after that, remembering Marie meant nothing to me. I wasn't interested in her dead. That seemed perfectly normal to me, since I understood very well that people would forget me when I was dead. They wouldn't have anything more to do with me. I wasn't even able to tell myself that it was hard to think those things.

It was at that exact moment that the chaplain came in. When I saw him I felt a little shudder go through me. He noticed it and told me not to be afraid. I told him that it wasn't his usual time. He replied that it was just a friendly visit and had nothing to do with my appeal, which he knew nothing about. He sat down on my bunk and invited me to sit next to him. I refused. All the same, there was something very gentle about him.

He sat there for a few seconds, leaning forward, with his elbows on his knees, looking at his hands. They were slender and sinewy and they reminded me of two nimble animals. He slowly rubbed one against the other. Then he sat there, leaning forward like that, for so long

4 **writing** 手紙を書くこと　5 **gotten tired of** うんざりする　7 **These things happen** そういうことは起こるものだ　8 **apart from our two bodies** われわれの体を別にすれば　12 **her dead** 死んでいる彼女　13 **normal** 自然　14 **wouldn't have anything more to do with me** それ以上、私に関わり合うことはない　18 **shudder** 身ぶるい　20 **his usual time** 彼がいつもやってくる時間　23 **bunk** 作り付けのベッド　**All the same** それなのに　27 **sinewy** 筋っぽい　28 **nimble** すばしこい

that for an instant I seemed to forget he was there.

But suddenly he raised his head and looked straight at me. "Why have you refused to see me?" he asked. I said that I didn't believe in God. He wanted to know if I was sure and I said that I didn't see any reason to ask myself that question: it seemed unimportant. He then leaned back against the wall, hands flat on his thighs. Almost as if it wasn't me he was talking to, he remarked that sometimes we think we're sure when in fact we're not. I didn't say anything. He looked at me and asked, "What do you think?" I said it was possible. In any case, I may not have been sure about what really did interest me, but I was absolutely sure about what didn't. And it just so happened that what he was talking about didn't interest me.

He looked away and without moving asked me if I wasn't talking that way out of extreme despair. I explained to him that I wasn't desperate. I was just afraid, which was only natural. "Then God can help you," he said. "Every man I have known in your position has turned to Him." I acknowledged that that was their right. It also meant that they must have had the time for it. As for me, I didn't want anybody's help, and I just didn't have the time to interest myself in what didn't interest me.

At that point he threw up his hands in annoyance but then sat forward and smoothed out the folds of his cassock. When he had finished he started in again, addressing me as "my friend." If he was talking to me this way,

6 **leaned back against the wall** 壁にもたれかかった 7 **hands flat on his thighs** 両手をぺったり膝に置いて 8 **as if it wasn't me he was talking to** 彼が話しかけているのは私ではないとでもいうように **remarked** いった 9 **we think we're sure when in fact we're not** われわれは、確信していないときでも、確信していると思う 13 **what didn't** = what really didn't interest me **it just so happened** たまたま that 以下のようなことになった
16 **looked away** 目をそらした 17 **talking that way** そんなふうに話している **out of extreme despair** 心から絶望しているせいで 18 **desperate** 絶望している 20 **in your position** あなたの置かれている状況 21 **turned to Him** 神に頼った **acknowledged** 認めた
26 **threw up his hands** 両手を上げた（あきらめた） **in annoyance** いらいらして 27 **sat forward** 前かがみになった **smoothed out the folds of his cassock** 法衣のシワを伸ばした
28 **addressing** 呼びかける

it wasn't because I was condemned to die; the way he saw it, we were all condemned to die. But I interrupted him by saying that it wasn't the same thing and that besides, it wouldn't be a consolation anyway. "Certainly," he agreed. "But if you don't die today, you'll die tomorrow, or the next day. And then the same question will arise. How will you face that terrifying ordeal?" I said I would face it exactly as I was facing it now.

At that he stood up and looked me straight in the eye. It was a game I knew well. I played it a lot with Emmanuel and Céleste and usually they were the ones who looked away. The chaplain knew the game well too, I could tell right away: his gaze never faltered. And his voice didn't falter, either, when he said, "Have you no hope at all? And do you really live with the thought that when you die, you die, and nothing remains?" "Yes," I said.

Then he lowered his head and sat back down. He told me that he pitied me. He thought it was more than a man could bear. I didn't feel anything except that he was beginning to annoy me. Then I turned away and went and stood under the skylight. I leaned my shoulder against the wall. Without really following what he was saying, I heard him start asking me questions again. He was talking in an agitated, urgent voice. I could see that he was genuinely upset, so I listened more closely.

He was expressing his certainty that my appeal would be granted, but I was carrying the burden of a sin from which I had to free myself. According to him, human

2 **we were all condemned to die** われわれはすべて死刑囚のようなものだ　4 **consolation** 慰め　7 **face** 面と向かう　**ordeal** 試練（死刑）

9 **At that** それをきいて　12 **I could tell right away** 私にはすぐにわかった　13 **never faltered** ゆらぐことはなかった

19 **it was more than a man could bear** 人間に耐えられることではなかった　22 **leaned my shoulder against the wall** 肩を壁にくっつけてもたれた　23 **following** 理解する　25 **an agitated, urgent voice** 興奮した、切迫した声　26 **genuinely** 本当に　**upset** 動揺している

29 **I had to free myself** 自分を（the burden of a sin「罪の重荷」から）解放しなくてはならない

justice was nothing and divine justice was everything. I pointed out that it was the former that had condemned me. His response was that it hadn't washed away my sin for all that. I told him I didn't know what a sin was. All they had told me was that I was guilty. I was guilty, I was paying for it, and nothing more could be asked of me. At that point he stood up again, and the thought occurred to me that in such a narrow cell, if he wanted to move around he didn't have many options. He could either sit down or stand up.

I was staring at the ground. He took a step toward me and stopped, as if he didn't dare come any closer. He looked at the sky through the bars. "You're wrong, my son," he said. "More could be asked of you. And it may be asked." "And what's that?" "You could be asked to see." "See what?"

The priest gazed around my cell and answered in a voice that sounded very weary to me. "Every stone here sweats with suffering, I know that. I have never looked at them without a feeling of anguish. But deep in my heart I know that the most wretched among you have seen a divine face emerge from their darkness. That is the face you are asked to see."

This perked me up a little. I said I had been looking at the stones in these walls for months. There wasn't anything or anyone in the world I knew better. Maybe at one time, way back, I had searched for a face in them. But the face I was looking for was as bright as the sun and the flame of desire—and it belonged to Marie. I had

2 **former** 前者（human justice） 4 **for all that** それにもかかわらず、結局は 6 **paying for it** つぐなっている、その代償を払っている **could be asked of me** 私に要求できる
12 **didn't dare come any closer** これ以上は近づくことができない 13 **bars** 格子
19 **sweats with suffering** 苦しみのせいで汗をかいている
20 **anguish** 苦悩 21 **the most wretched** 最もみじめな人間
22 **emerge** 現れる、浮かび上がる **their darkness** 彼らの闇
24 **perked me up a little** 少し元気になった 25 **There wasn't anything or anyone in the world I knew better** 私はこれほどよく知っている物もなければ人もいない 27 **way back** かつて
29 **flame of desire** 欲望の炎 **it belonged to Marie** それはマリーの顔だった

searched for it in vain. Now it was all over. And in any case, I'd never seen anything emerge from any sweating stones.

The chaplain looked at me with a kind of sadness. I now had my back flat against the wall, and light was streaming over my forehead. He muttered a few words I didn't catch and abruptly asked if he could embrace me. "No," I said. He turned and walked over to the wall and slowly ran his hand over it. "Do you really love this earth as much as all that?" he murmured. I didn't answer.

He stood there with his back to me for quite a long time. His presence was grating and oppressive. I was just about to tell him to go, to leave me alone, when all of a sudden, turning toward me, he burst out, "No, I refuse to believe you! I know that at one time or another you've wished for another life." I said of course I had, but it didn't mean any more than wishing to be rich, to be able to swim faster, or to have a more nicely shaped mouth. It was all the same. But he stopped me and wanted to know how I pictured this other life. Then I shouted at him, "One where I could remember this life!" and that's when I told him I'd had enough. He wanted to talk to me about God again, but I went up to him and made one last attempt to explain to him that I had only a little time left and I didn't want to waste it on God. He tried to change the subject by asking me why I was calling him "monsieur" and not "father." That got me mad, and I told him he wasn't my father; he wasn't even on

9 **ran his hand over it** 手で壁をなでた　10 **as much as all that** そんな考えでいるのに
13 **grating** 神経に障る　**oppressive** 鬱陶しい　14 **leave me alone** 私をひとりにする　15 **burst out** 激しい調子で話しだした　16 **at one time or another** いつか、いつとはいえないが　18 **didn't mean any more than** than 以下のことと同じだ　22 **One where I could remember this life!** One は Life。この人生を思い出すことができるような人生　23 **I'd had enough** もう十分だ、もう帰ってくれ　25 **I had only a little time left** あとわずかな時間しか残されていない　26 **I didn't want to waste it on God** 神のことなんかでその時間をむだにしたくない　27 **calling him "monsieur" and not "father."** 相手を「ムシュ」と呼んで､｢父｣と呼ばない　28 **That got me mad** それをきいて、私はかっとなった

my side.

"Yes, my son," he said, putting his hand on my shoulder, "I am on your side. But you have no way of knowing it, because your heart is blind. I shall pray for you."

Then, I don't know why, but something inside me snapped. I started yelling at the top of my lungs, and I insulted him and told him not to waste his prayers on me. I grabbed him by the collar of his cassock. I was pouring out on him everything that was in my heart, cries of anger and cries of joy. He seemed so certain about everything, didn't he? And yet none of his certainties was worth one hair of a woman's head. He wasn't even sure he was alive, because he was living like a dead man. Whereas it looked as if I was the one who'd come up emptyhanded. But I was sure about me, about everything, surer than he could ever be, sure of my life and sure of the death I had waiting for me. Yes, that was all I had. But at least I had as much of a hold on it as it had on me. I had been right, I was still right, I was always right. I had lived my life one way and I could just as well have lived it another. I had done this and I hadn't done that. I hadn't done this thing but I had done another. And so? It was as if I had waited all this time for this moment and for the first light of this dawn to be vindicated. Nothing, nothing mattered, and I knew why. So did he. Throughout the whole absurd life I'd lived, a dark wind had been rising toward me from somewhere deep in my future, across years that were still to come, and as it passed, this wind leveled whatever was offered

2 **Yes** Yes, I'm your father 3 **you have no way of knowing it** あなたにはそれがわからない
6 **snapped** 音を立てて折れた 7 **not to waste his prayers on me** 私のためにに祈るようなむだなことはするな 8 **grabbed him by the collar of his cassock** 司祭の法衣の襟をつかんだ 10 **He seemed...**（ここからあと、p244の21行目までは、主人公が司祭にむかって怒鳴る言葉） **certain about everything** すべてのことに確信がある 11 **And yet** しかし 14 **Whereas** それに対して、一方 15 **come up emptyhanded** 手に何も持っていない状態になっている 18 **I had as much of a hold on it** 自分はそれをしっかりつかんでいる 19 **as it had on me** それが私をしっかりつかんでいるように 20 **lived my life one way** こんな人生を生きてきた **I could just as well have lived it another** ほかの人生を生きることもできた 25 **vindicated** 正しいと証明される 26 **So did he.** = He also knew why. **Throughout the whole absurd life I've lived** 私が生きてきたこの不条理な（ばかばかしい）人生すべてにおいて **a dark wind had been rising toward me** 黒い風が私のほうに吹きつけていた 27 **from somewhere deep in my future** 私の未来のどこか深いところから 28 **across years that were still to come** これからくるべき（未来の）時間を通って 29 **as it passed** その風は通りすぎるときに **leveled** ならしてしまう、一様にしてしまう **whatever was offered to me** 私に差しだされたものをすべて

to me at the time, in years no more real than the ones I was living. What did other people's deaths or a mother's love matter to me; what did his God or the lives people choose or the fate they think they elect matter to me when we're all elected by the same fate, me and billions of privileged people like him who also called themselves my brothers? Couldn't he see, couldn't he see that? Everybody was privileged. There were only privileged people. The others would all be condemned one day. And he would be condemned, too. What would it matter if he were accused of murder and then executed because he didn't cry at his mother's funeral? Salamano's dog was worth just as much as his wife. The little robot woman was just as guilty as the Parisian woman Masson married, or as Marie, who had wanted me to marry her. What did it matter that Raymond was as much my friend as Céleste, who was worth a lot more than him? What did it matter that Marie now offered her lips to a new Meursault? Couldn't he, couldn't this condemned man see . . . And that from somewhere deep in my future . . . All the shouting had me gasping for air. But they were already tearing the chaplain from my grip and the guards were threatening me. He calmed them, though, and looked at me for a moment without saying anything. His eyes were full of tears. Then he turned and disappeared.

With him gone, I was able to calm down again. I was exhausted and threw myself on my bunk. I must have fallen asleep, because I woke up with the stars in my

1 **years no more real than the ones I was living** 私が生きている時間と同じくらい現実感のない時間　3 **what did his God or the lives people choose or the fate they think they elect matter to me**（matter の主部は his God...elect まで全部）彼の神や、生きている人間が選んだ人生や、彼らが選んだつもりでいる運命など、私になんの関係があるだろう　5 **when we're all elected by the same fate** われわれみんなが同じ運命に選ばれているときに　**me and billions of privileged people like him** 私も、彼のような特権化された何十億人もの人々も　7 **Couldn't he see, couldn't he see that?**（he は司祭）あんたにはわからないのか、あんたにはそれがわからないのか？　19 **a new Meursault** 新しいムルソー　**Couldn't he, couldn't this condemned man see**（he は司祭）あんたにはわからないのか、（私と同様）死ぬべき運命のあんたにはわからないのか？　21 **in my future . . .** ここまで、主人公が司祭にむかって怒鳴る言葉　**All the shouting had me gasping for air** 叫びつづけてきて、私は苦しくてあえいでいる　22 **they were already tearing the chaplain from my grip** 彼らはすでに私の手から司祭を引き離していた
23 **calmed**　なだめた
28 **threw myself** ベッドに転がった　29 **with the stars in my face** 顔を星明かりが照らしている

face. Sounds of the countryside were drifting in. Smells of night, earth, and salt air were cooling my temples. The wondrous peace of that sleeping summer flowed through me like a tide. Then, in the dark hour before dawn, sirens blasted. They were announcing departures for a world that now and forever meant nothing to me. For the first time in a long time I thought about Maman. I felt as if I understood why at the end of her life she had taken a "fiancé," why she had played at beginning again. Even there, in that home where lives were fading out, evening was a kind of wistful respite. So close to death, Maman must have felt free then and ready to live it all again. Nobody, nobody had the right to cry over her. And I felt ready to live it all again too. As if that blind rage had washed me clean, rid me of hope; for the first time, in that night alive with signs and stars, I opened myself to the gentle indifference of the world. Finding it so much like myself—so like a brother, really—I felt that I had been happy and that I was happy again. For everything to be consummated, for me to feel less alone, I had only to wish that there be a large crowd of spectators the day of my execution and that they greet me with cries of hate.

1 **were drifting in** 流れこんでいた 3 **wondrous peace** すばらしい安らぎ **sleeping summer** 眠っている夏 4 **like a tide** 潮のように 5 **blasted** 響きわたった **departures for a world** 新しい世界への出発 6 **now and forever meant nothing to me** 今もこれからも、私にとっては意味のない 9 **taken a "fiancé"** 婚約した **why she had played at beginning again** なぜ母親がたわむれに再び人生を始めたのか 10 **lives were fading out** 生が消えていく 11 **wistful respite** 切ない休息 13 **nobody had the right to cry over her** だれにも母親のために泣く権利はない、母親をかわいそうに思うべきではない 15 **blind rage** 激しい怒り **rid me of hope** 私から希望を払拭した、取りあげた 16 **in that night alive with signs and stars** 予兆と星が息づいているこの夜 17 **I opened myself to the gentle indifference of the world** 私は世界のやさしい無関心を受け入れた 20 **For everything to be consummated** すべてが完成されるためには **for me to feel less alone** 私が孤独でなくなるためには 21 **I had only to wish that** that 以下のことを望みさえすればいい **there be a large crowd of spectators** 大勢の見物人がやってくる 22 **the day of my execution** 私の処刑の日に **they greet me with cries of hate** 憎悪の叫びで私を迎える

あとがき

1913年（大正2年)、この年に生まれた作家、学者、役者、写真家には、織田作之助、新美南吉、、アルフレッド·ベスター、金田一春彦、森繁久彌、ロバート·キャパなどがいる。そんな人々のうちのひとり、アルベール・カミュ（1913年～1960年）は25、6歳の頃、アフリカのフランス領アルジェリアで、こんな小説を書こうと考えていた。

タイトルはL'etranger。英語ではThe Stranger。日本語訳では『異邦人』となっているが、このフランス語、英語には「見知らぬ人、よそ者、他人、訪問者、門外漢」など色々な意味がある。

主人公のムルソーが海岸でアラブ人を射殺した罪で起訴され、死刑を宣告されるという内容だ。この小説は1942年に出版され、カミュは一躍、フランス文壇に躍りでる。じつに新鮮でショッキングな作品だったのだ。そして次々に他国でも翻訳出版されるようになり、世界的なベストセラー、ロングセラーになる。世界が驚きと感動の拍手を送った作品だ。

カミュはその後、『シーシュポスの神話』『ペスト』などを発表し、1957年、ノーベル文学賞を受賞。1905年生まれのジャン・ポール・サルトル（1964年、ノーベル文学賞を拒否）とともに、戦後のフランス文学を代表する作家となった。

とくにカミュの代表作『異邦人』は今でもファンが

多い。

たとえば、

・新潮社の「考える人」という雑誌の2008年春号の特集「海外の長篇小説ベスト100」という、識者129名の投票によるリストで17位。

・ルモンド紙＋書店チェーンＦＮＡＣ主催「20世紀の名作ベスト50」（1999年）では1位。

・イギリス、アイルランド、ヨーロッパに200以上の店舗を持つ本の大型チェーン店である〈ウォーターストーン〉が行った「20世紀の作品ベスト100」という、2万5千人以上の投票では20位。

といった具合だ。

とにかく、この『異邦人』、20世紀を代表する作品といっていい。

20世紀、この作品のキーワードは「不条理」（英訳では'absurd'という単語がそれにあたる）といわれた。日本語訳の文庫本の裏にも「不条理の認識を極度に追求したカミュの代表作」と書かれている。不条理の認識というと妙に難しくきこえるが、簡単にまとめてしまえば、「人間の生はなんの意味もなく、不条理なのだ」ということだ。

実際、最後のほうで司祭に "Have you no hope at all? And do you really live with the thought that when you die, you die, and nothing remains?"（では、まったく希望を持っていないのですか？　本当に、死ぬときは、死ぬのであって、何も残らないと思っているのですか？）ときかれ、ムルソーは "Yes," と答える。

ムルソーが最後にいきついた認識はどんなものなのか、彼はどんな気持ちで死に臨むことにしたのか、そのへんは各自、読んで考えてみてほしい。

もしかしたら、21世紀、これを読む若い人たちは、「不条理」とかいわれてもピンとこないかもしれない。それはそれでいいと思う。

ぼくは今回、英語版で読み直してみて、じつによく書けた現代リアリズム小説だなと思った。

母親の葬式であまり悲しまず、そのすぐあとで、かわいい女の子と泳ぎにいったり、いわくのありそうな知り合いと飲んだあげく、暑い暑い砂漠でアラブ人を撃ち殺してしまった男の気持ちが、とても自然に伝わってくるし、母親の葬儀のときの態度が裁判のときに批判され、追求されて、死刑を宣告される主人公に、どこか共感してしまった。

とくに、エンディング近くの彼の心情は激しく、切なく迫ってくる。

70年前に出版されたとき、なんでそんなに世界が驚いたのだろうと不思議になったくらいだ。しかし、それは『異邦人』が第2次世界大戦後の新しい小説として世界中で広く読まれ、その影響を受けた作品が次々に生まれた結果なのかもしれない。

そんなことも考えながら読んでみると、またこの作品の新しい魅力が発見できるかもしれない。

金原瑞人

［著者］

アルベール・カミュ　Albert Camus

フランスの小説家、劇作家。1913年–1960年。フランス領アルジェリア出身。アルジェ大学卒業後ジャーナリストとして活動、第二次大戦中に刊行された小説『異邦人』、エッセイ『シーシュポスの神話』などで注目される。戦後に発表した小説『ペスト』はベストセラーに。1957年、史上二番目の若さでノーベル文学賞を受賞。サルトルとともに戦後のフランス文学を代表する作家となった。カミュの著作は「不条理」という概念によって特徴付けられている。1960年、交通事故により急死。

［編者］

金原瑞人（かねはら・みずひと）

法政大学教授、翻訳家。ヤングアダルト小説をはじめ海外文学の紹介、翻訳で著名。著書『翻訳のさじかげん』（ポプラ社）ほか。訳書『豚の死なない日』（ロバート・ニュートン・ペック、白水社）『青空のむこう』（アレックス・シアラー、求龍堂）『国のない男』（カート・ヴォネガット、ＮＨＫ出版）ほか多数。編著『金原瑞人 MY FAVORITES　THE BOX』（ブルース・コウヴィル、青灯社）。

金原瑞人 MY FAVORITES
異邦人 THE STRANGER

2012年11月30日　第1刷発行
2023年10月31日　第2刷発行

著者　アルベール・カミュ

編者　金原瑞人

発行者　辻一三

発行所　株式会社青灯社
東京都新宿区新宿 1-4-13
郵便番号 160-0022
電話 03-5368-6923（編集）
03-5368-6550（販売）
URL http://www.seitosha-p.co.jp
振替　00120-8-260856

印刷・製本　モリモト印刷株式会社

ISBN978-4-86228-063-3 C0082

小社ロゴは、田中恭吉「ろうそく」（和歌山県立近代美術館所蔵）をもとに、菊地信義氏が作成